10 ▶ TRUTHS about SOCIALISM

D. JAMES
KENNEDY
MINISTRIES

FORT LAUDERDALE, FL

TEN TRUTHS ABOUT SOCIALISM

ISBN: 978-1-929626-64-9

Cover and Interior Design: Roark Creative, **www.roarkcreative.com**

Published by D. James Kennedy Ministries

Printed in the United States of America

D. James Kennedy Ministries
P.O. Box 11786, Fort Lauderdale, FL 33339
1-800-988-7884
DJKM.org
letters@djkm.org

CONTENTS

CONTENTS

SOCIALISM

"Any of various economic and political theories advocating collective or governmental ownership and administration of the means of production and distribution of goods."

Merriam-Webster's Collegiate Dictionary (Eleventh Edition)

SHORT DEFINITION

"Legalized plunder."

Frederic Bastiat, *The Law*, 1848

SOCIALISM HAS FAILED WHEREVER IT HAS BEEN TRIED. SO WHY IS AMERICA TURNING TOWARD THIS BANKRUPT IDEA?

INTRODUCTION

"We've Never Seen Anything Like This Before"

After seventy years and the death of millions, the prison-house of communism burst open almost three decades ago with the collapse of the Berlin Wall on November 9, 1989. Jubilant East Germans streamed into West Berlin where, in a festival of freedom, they joined their West German counterparts in breaking up the massive concrete divider with sledgehammers. Communist regimes in Czechoslovakia, Romania, Bulgaria, and Albania all soon fell, as did the Soviet Union itself. The Union of Soviet Socialist Republics was dissolved and landed on the ash heap of history on Christmas Day 1991.

Socialism* was in full rout. In the late 1970s, socialist regimes had commanded the allegiance of some 60 percent of all people on earth. Socialism's spectacular crash in the years that followed signaled to many that this tragic and bloody experiment was at long last over. Historian Joshua Muravchik offered an epitaph for it in his 2002 review of the "rise and fall of socialism:"

> Within a couple decades, socialism was officially repealed in half the places where it had triumphed. In the other half, it continued in name only. Today, in but a few flyspecks on the

*The term "socialism" is used interchangeably with "communism" throughout this book. While some stipulate distinctions, the two terms both refer to a system of coerced common ownership in which economic decisions are made by central government planners and not private individuals or corporations.

map is there still an earnest effort to practice socialism, defended in the manner of those marooned Japanese soldiers who held out for decades after 1945, never having learned that their emperor had surrendered.[1]

Spreading the Wealth

Then came 2008. First, President George W. Bush "abandoned free-market principles," as he later put it, by pledging taxpayer money to bail out Wall Street and Detroit. Next came the election of Barack Obama, who famously told Joe "the Plumber" Wurzelbacher that "when you spread the wealth around, it's good for everybody."

A crowd at the Berlin Wall waits to celebrate the opening of the Brandenburg Gate in Berlin, December 22, 1989. The first Berlin Wall border opening came November 9, 1989. (Newscom)

Once in office, President Obama began to fulfill his campaign promise of "fundamentally transforming the United States." Within months, GM and Chrysler were annexed to Uncle Sam, salary caps were placed on Wall Street executives whose banks took bail-out funds, and a $789 billion package of government spending to spur economic growth passed Congress.

And then the President, with the aid of Democratic leadership in the House and Senate, began the long march to place America's health care system under federal oversight and control.

The President detailed his economic philosophy in his 2009 budget statement, "A New Era of Responsibility: Renewing America's Promise."

> For the better part of three decades, a disproportionate share of the Nation's wealth has been accumulated by the very wealthy. Technological advances and growing global competition, while transforming whole industries — and birthing new ones — has accentuated the trend toward rising inequality.[2]

It was time, the President declared, "to break from a troubled past" and "begin charting a new path" — a path of increased government intervention and control of the private economy.

What Mr. Obama was doing, *Wall Street Journal* columnist Daniel Henninger wrote, was "proposing that the U.S. government both guide the economy … and do so with a new, aggressively redistributive tax policy."[3]

The near-term result, Rep. Michele Bachmann (MN-R) told this ministry in February 2010, is that some 30 percent of private industry has now come under federal control. With the passage of Obamacare, another 18 percent of our economy is now controlled by the federal government. As Bachmann noted, "We've never seen anything like this before."[4]

Well, actually, we have. Maybe not in the U.S., but after more than 150 years of theory and practice, socialism is very much a known quantity. The bitter experience of millions offers ample evidence that collective ownership is just what one free market economist called it in the 1940s — "the road to serfdom."[5]

The pages that follow reveal the record of socialism in lives lost, freedoms taken, and economies ruined. It shows how the envy-inflamed ideas of Marx, Engels, Lenin, et al., are at war with the family, the Church, and with God and His Word.

It's a post-mortem on what Muravchik called "man's most ambitious attempt to supplant religion with a doctrine about how life ought to be lived." And it's a warning to Americans not to let this failed idea take hold and bring ruin to our nation.

President Barack Obama
(Zuma)

TRUTH 1

Socialism Was The Wrong Response To Real Problems

"Man was born free and everywhere he is in chains."
— Jean-Jacques Rousseau, *The Social Contract* (1762)

"Let the ruling classes tremble at a Communist revolution. The proletarians have nothing to lose, but their chains. They have a world to win. Working men of all countries, unite!"
— Karl Marx and Friedrich Engels, *The Communist Manifesto* (1847)

Hints of socialism can be found as early as the ancient Greeks, but the development of a cohesive philosophy of socialism began just before the French and American revolutions, mostly as a response to the beginnings of the Industrial Age.

Until that time, most economic activity was confined to the home, the farm, and small enterprises. Spurred by technology, science, manufacturing, and trade, new industries arose that required more labor. This resulted in more goods, more services, and more need for people to work outside the home.

In Europe, factories employed thousands of men, women, and children, often at long hours, low wages, and sometimes in horrific conditions.

Jean-Jacques Rousseau
(American Vision)

Economic disparities became more pronounced, with a rising wealthy business class, a burgeoning labor class, and a still-embryonic middle class.

As authors Albert Fried and Ronald Sanders document in their book, *Socialist Thought*, "[U]nlike classical liberalism…Socialism was a reaction *against* the industrial revolution," with its "laissez faire" (hands off) economics.[6]

The English political philosopher Thomas Hobbes (1588-1679) pioneered the idea of the "social contract," in which people gave up many freedoms in return for security from the ruling authority. His book *Leviathan* (1651) made the case that without a strong central authority backed by the people themselves, life in a state of nature would be "solitary, poor, nasty, brutish and short."

George Wilhelm Friedrich Hegel

Later, John Locke (1632-1704), whom many of America's Founding Fathers used as a source of ideas, applied the Hobbesian theory of rights secured through the social contract, but tempered it with the Christian understanding that man, created in the image of God, had a moral sense and thus, certain rights. His conception of "government with the consent of the governed" was a driving force behind America's Declaration of Independence, rooted in unalienable rights created by "nature and nature's God."

Political philosophers such as the Germans Immanuel Kant (1724-1804), and George Wilhelm Friedrich Hegel (1770-1831) and the Frenchmen Voltaire and Rousseau began reassessing assumptions about God, knowledge, truth, and social and economic structures in the eighteenth century. Kant argued, among other things, that knowledge is subjective. Hegel pronounced that "the rational alone is real" and described a "dialectic" in which history unfolds as a process.

Later, Karl Marx (1818-1883) incorporated Hegel's dialectic and expanded it into "dialectical materialism," a philosophical system based on Hegel's appropriation of the Greek philosopher Socrates' dialogues, in which a thesis is countered by an anti-thesis, resulting in a synthesis. Marx recast history as a series of ever-evolving syntheses of economic class warfare, with capitalism as the final major stage before "the dictatorship of the proletariat" and communism.

In his classic treatises, *Discourse on the Origin of Inequality* (1754) and *The Social Contract* (1762), Rousseau argued that man was more virtuous and free at one time in a state of nature, that society and property ownership had corrupted him, and that the only solution was a powerful state that owned all property and enforced absolute equality.[7] Rousseau's secular view that man would be good, absent the temptations of power and privilege, conflicted directly with Hobbes' low view of humanity and also with the biblical view that man is inherently flawed and has been since The Fall in the Garden of Eden.

Like Rousseau, most of the *Philosophes* of France's Enlightenment rejected the doctrine of Original Sin.[8] Perhaps the biggest flaw in socialism is its misreading of human nature, particularly the role that the sin of envy plays. For some reason, socialists seem to forget that government authorities are just as vulnerable to the corrupting influence of envy — wanting what is not yours — as the general populace.

Two Revolutions With Different Consequences

As socialist doctrines simmered, two revolutions occurred in the late eighteenth century that had far-reaching and quite different outcomes. The American Revolution (1776-1781) was fought to restore the rights of the colonists as free Englishmen under English Common Law, which was based on biblical principles, as explained by the great English lawyer William Blackstone. Government was limited, and property rights were protected. America's Founders went on to form a government based on a biblical view of human nature. Since man cannot be trusted, they reasoned, no man or men should be given great power over their fellow men.

Thus, the Constitution deliberately created a separation of powers and checks and balances within the national government and between the states and the national government, and guarantees property rights, the freedoms of religion, speech, assembly and redress, and the right to bear arms. The great flaw was allowing slavery, which eventually tore the nation apart and was not resolved until the War Between the States (1861-1865). It took another 100 years and the civil rights movement to secure full rights for African Americans. Meanwhile, the economy soared, survived the Great Depression, and America became the world leader in wealth, military power, and influence.

Karl Marx
(American Vision)

Marx predicted that the "masses" would overthrow governments and create a "dictatorship of the proletariat," beginning in the industrialized nations.

On the other side of the Atlantic, the Rousseauean vision of man as perfectable in a collective state took hold. The French Revolution (1789) was a revolt not only against capitalism and royalty, but was also an anti-Christian revolution that soon turned on its own, with guillotines dispatching first the privileged and then anyone thought to be insufficiently revolutionary. The revolution was supposed to usher in an Age of Reason, but instead fomented the chaos that allowed Napoleon to take ultimate power and to plunge Europe into war.

Various utopian, anarchist, and socialist thinkers dominated French philosophy during the nineteenth century, paving the way for a German, Karl Marx, who co-authored *The Communist Manifesto* (1847), which condemned free markets, capitalism, and "inequality." Marx predicted that the "masses" would overthrow governments and create a "dictatorship of the proletariat," beginning in the industrialized nations. The state would eventually fade away into a "classless society" as men became altruistic.

In 1848 and 1849, anarchists and socialists launched failed revolutions in Europe. Marx's vision of an international socialist movement sweeping all nations under a regime of absolute equality was stalled. But with assistance from Friedrich Engels (1820-1895), Marx wrote another major book *Das Kapital* (1867), and his ideas continued to spread throughout Europe.

Some socialist thinkers, such as Robert Owen (1771-1858) arose in England, but Great Britain also had its share of profoundly influential free-market thinkers, such as John Locke (1632-1704), Scotland's Adam Smith (1723-1790) and Edmund Burke (1729-1797), all of whom influenced America's founding fathers.

Paving the Way for Communism and Nazism

After decades of rapid industrial growth and relative stability, Europe plunged into World War I (1914-1918), which shattered the monarchial oligarchies and opened Russia up to the Bolshevik Revolution in October 1917. Communists, led by Vladimir Lenin (1870-1924), finally had a country of their own to demonstrate the superiority of their international socialist vision. But Lenin found he had to suppress "counter-revolutionaries" who resented the crackdown on churches and civil rights and the seizure and redistribution of property. Nothing less than total war was warranted. Lenin wrote:

> The dictatorship of the proletariat is a stubborn struggle — bloody and bloodless, violent and peaceful, military and economic, educational and administrative —against the forces and traditions of the old society.[9]

Soon, the prisons and graveyards of the new Soviet Union were filled with dissenters, paving the way for the reign of Joseph Stalin (1878-1953), who developed his own "socialism in one country" and murdered millions in the name of equality.[10]

Over in Marx's Germany, a young socialist named Adolf Hitler (1889-1945) wrote his own manifesto in 1925 and 1926, the two-volume *Mein Kampf* (*My Struggle*), and picked up the pieces of a war-torn, defeated Germany. He built a National Socialist German Workers Party, and the Nazis took over Germany in 1933, when Hitler became Chancellor. Proclaiming the creation of a thousand-year Third Reich, Hitler targeted the Jews for extinction and created a massive military machine that plunged the world into World War II (1939-1945).[11] Meanwhile, in Italy, Benito Mussolini rose to power on his version of socialism, which was called Fascism. The Fascists, like the Nazis, allowed some private ownership of industrial production, closely managed by party bureaucrats.[12]

Both the Nazi-Fascist version of socialism and the Communist Party version emphasized the primacy of the state over the individual, the family, and the Church, along with the state's

Adolf Hitler

ultimate control of property, the crushing of dissent, and control of the press. They were two sides of the same coin, even though they bitterly hated each other, with National Socialism vying with International Socialism (Communism) for domination. A common myth perpetuated in academia and the media is that a straight line axis would put the Nazis on the far right and the communists on the far left, with America somewhere in between. But the communists and Nazis are both, in fact, on the far left of the axis. On the far right would be anarchists who believe in no government. America, with its limited government and guarantees of individual liberty, would be somewhere in between.

Right Diagnosis, Wrong Solution
The rise of socialism did not happen in a spurt of intellectual fantasy. It was a direct reaction to industrial capitalism, which radically altered societal institutions right down to the fam-

ily. The Christian author Charles Dickens (1812-1870) painted especially evocative portraits of the suffering lower classes' 12- to 14-hour work days and child factory labor.

But the suffering and dislocation brought about by industrialization also yielded a startling increase in wealth. Historian Joshua Muravchik reports that per capita income in England and Germany doubled between 1848 and 1899.[13] That increase benefited all sectors of society.

Marx and his collaborator Friedrich Engels correctly deduced that the dynamic economics of capitalism would pose a challenge to the traditional family, since it required family members to spend so much time away from each other, especially fathers in the workplace. In *The Communist Manifesto*, Marx wrote:

> The bourgeois clap-trap about the family and education, about the hallowed co-relation of parent and child, becomes all the more disgusting, the more, by the action of Modern Industry, all family ties among the proletarians are torn asunder, and their children transformed into simple articles of commerce and instruments of labour.[14]

Marx saw this as the advent of even more radical change, declaring war on religion and family as obstacles to progress toward communism:

> On what foundation is the present family,
> the bourgeois family, based? On capital, on
> private gain. In its completely developed form
> this family exists only among the bourgeoisie.
> But this state of things finds its complement in
> the practical absence of the family among the
> proletarians, and in public prostitution. The
> bourgeois family will vanish as a manner of
> course when its complement vanishes, and
> both will vanish with the vanishing of capital.[15]

The most prominent socialist thinkers, including Engels, promoted the sexual revolution in which marriage and family were devalued in order to eliminate loyalties other than to the state.[16]

It's no coincidence that today's socialists and progressives support not only more government power and redistribution schemes, but every aspect of the sexual revolution—from the spread of pornography, to abortion, homosexuality, and the legal assault on marriage. All of it works toward empowering the state at the expense of family and church.[17]

Great Britain and America, fortified by a vibrant Christian culture, were able to withstand the siren song of socialism until the latter portion of the twentieth century. Europe, by contrast, flirted with every possible variety in a vain effort to improve social conditions. The twentieth century became the bloodiest century in history, as Nazi Germany and the Soviet Union perpetrated genocide and unspeakable horrors upon their own people and other nations. The Marxist virus spread to China, where Mao Tse-tung's communist regime murdered tens of millions, and led to Cambodia's killing fields. Communist regimes from Cuba to East Germany oppressed their people in countless ways.

On the positive side, and a glaring rebuke to the false promises of socialism, the twentieth century is also known as "the American Century," since America became the wealthiest, freest, most powerful nation in history.

John Quincy Adams observed, "The highest glory of the American Revolution was this: it connected in one indissoluble bond, the principles of civil government with the precepts of Christianity."[18]

This is why America has been able to avoid many of the pitfalls plaguing socialist nations. As America has drifted from its Christian origins, however, it is showing signs of the same socialist disease: weak or non-existent faith in God and the Bible's wisdom, a rising obsession with materialism, commensurate loss of virtue in the people and respect for innocent life, and an ever-growing government to pick up the pieces. Unless America retraces its steps and reasserts its own spiritual heritage, it risks exchanging self-government for the false promises of a secular, socialist state.

Since the beginning of time, man has tried to replace God's authority with his own machinations, always with bad results. Socialism is man's prideful error on a gigantic scale:

"There is a way that seems right to a man, but its end is the way of death." — Proverbs 14:12

If Americans do not acknowledge their current prideful errors, they risk coming to such an end.

—Robert Knight

TRUTH 2

**Socialism's Founding
Fathers Rejected God**

Socialism is an attempt to create heaven on earth according to an ever-changing morality fashioned by men themselves. Socialists are generally at war with the past; they believe that all that came before must be forgotten or destroyed in order to build a new Socialist Man from the ashes. This puts socialism at war, first and foremost, with God and the Bible, and, indeed, with any religious faith that contains moral absolutes.

Downgrading the Deity

In Europe's Enlightenment period, many leading philosophers began putting man at the center of all things instead of God. Beyond challenging the economic system, the budding strains of socialism were a rebellion against the authority of churches and traditional moral norms. If man no longer had to answer to God, he could make up his own rules.

Thomas Hobbes (1588-1679), author of *Leviathan*, was no socialist, but he was "an atheistic materialist for whom humans were appetite-driven animals. For good or ill, that is exactly how modern man is trained to understand himself," writes Hobbes biographer Jeffrey Collins.[19] Hobbes' idea of the "social contract" between people and their rulers replacing the divine right of kings became a key component of Enlightenment political theory.

The advent of science, which thinkers like the devoutly Christian Sir Isaac Newton (1642-1727) regarded as a tool to study God's natural forces, soon became an end unto itself in the new order of materialism.

Sir Isaac Newton
(Library of Congress)

Francis Schaeffer observed that:

> Scientists in the seventeenth and eighteenth centuries continued to use the word God, but pushed God more and more to the edges of their systems. Finally, scientists in this stream of thought moved to the idea of a completely closed system. This left no room for God. But equally it left no room for man. Man disappears, to be viewed as some form of determined or behavioristic machine. Thinkers such as Jean-Jacques Rousseau (1712-1778) and Ludwig Feuerbach (1804-1872) converted this mechanistic view of man into a philosophy of life.[20]

Claude Henri Saint Simon (1760-1825) wrote "Letter from an Inhabitant of Geneva to His Contemporaries" in which he proposed in 1803 a world in which a scientific select few governed the world. His passion for a Plato-like regime of elites morphed into a plan to transform Christianity into what he called The New Christianity, based on a single idea:

All men must behave as brothers toward one another.

He proclaimed that "this sublime principle contains everything that is divine in the Christian religion."[21] That would be news to Jesus Christ, who, when asked what was God's greatest commandment, said:

> "You shall love the Lord your God with all your heart, with all your soul and with all your mind." This is the first and great commandment. And the second is like it: "You shall love your neighbor as yourself." On these two commandments hang all the Law and the Prophets (Matthew 22:37-40).

By cutting out God and emphasizing only human interaction, the early socialists began constructing systems aimed solely at raising the "poor classes" (and thus bringing down the rich). Many of them stopped pretending that their vision was merely an advanced form of Christianity and, like Karl Marx, embraced outright atheism.

James Billington, who later became Librarian of Congress, documented the rise of the "revolutionary faith" that challenged Christianity. He traced its origins to the Palais-Royal cafes of

Paris in the late eighteenth century, where, he noted, "Nowhere — the literal meaning of Utopia — first became somewhere."[22]

The free-wheeling salons of the Palais-Royal hatched all sorts of visions of human liberation, from the sexual to the political. Anarchists mixed with socialists and the early communists. The only rule was that the rules of civilization were suspended, and that traditional views of church and man were not welcome.

> The cafés provided not just a protected place for political meetings, but also the intoxicating ambiance of an earthly utopia. Distinctions of rank were obliterated, and men were free to exercise sexual as well as political freedom.... In such an atmosphere, illusion and fantasy mixed with material gratification and made the ideal of total secular happiness seem credible.[23]

Within a few years, the revolutionary ferment in the cafés boiled over into outright revolution in 1789. After Napoleon's rise, and then his fall in 1815, France returned to more traditional ways, but exploded in communist-inspired uprisings in 1848.

Meanwhile, in England, John Goodwyn Barmby (1820-1881) brought communist ideas back from Paris and tried to start an outright Church of Communism to replace Christianity.

Recognizing that man has an unquenchable desire for God, socialists like Barmby created a false religion of equality, borrowing religious imagery and terms.

> He wrote communist hymns and prayers.... He called himself "Pontifarch of the Communist Church," proclaimed the "religion of COMMUNISM," called for the rejection of Christ's claim to messiahship, and defined communism as a new fusion of Judaism with "Christianism."[24]

Billington notes that, "the French founders left behind a legacy of unalterable opposition to supernatural religion."

[Theodore] Dezamy's last three major works argued in the course of 1845-46 for a materialist and atheist worldview to supplant Catholicism for "the organization of universal well-being." Already in his prize essay of 1839, Dezamy had spoken of "this sublime devotion which constitutes socialism" and bid the "unhappy proletarians" ... "reenter in the gyre of the egalitarian church, outside of which there is no salvation."[25] For Dezamy — as for his admirer Karl Marx — the atheism of his mature years was ... an essential premise of his whole theory.[26]

Another influential writer, the Frenchman François-Marie Arouet, who wrote about social reform and many other topics under the pen name of Voltaire (1694-1778), considered himself a Deist. He believed in a divine intelligence, but not the God of the Bible, and became a fierce critic of the Church as well as Judaism.

In Great Britain, Robert Owen (1771-1858), an associate of Barmby, was an early proponent of socialism who bitterly attacked religion and argued that man is not responsible for his own will and actions, but is a product of his environment. You might say he was the original bleeding heart liberal who insists that criminals are not responsible for their actions. Owen took over a factory in New Lanark, Scotland, and introduced many reforms that did benefit the employees. He later established the utopian New Harmony community in Indiana, based on socialist principles of common ownership and

Robert Owen
(Indiana Historical Society)

control. The project collapsed in short order.[27] In his old age, Owen himself abandoned his materialistic outlook and became an advocate of spiritualism, the occult practice of contacting the dead through mediums.[28]

In Germany, Friedrich Engels debated friends concerning the authority of Scripture and the New Testament claim that Jesus died for humanity's sins. In 1839, he pronounced himself a "child of God," but a skeptic nonetheless, in a letter to a friend:

> I cannot understand how one can still try to maintain literal belief in the Bible or defend the direct influence of God, since this cannot be proved anywhere.... I readily admit that I am a sinner and that I have a deep-rooted propensity to sin... but, my dear Fritz, no thinking person can believe that my sins can be remitted by the merits of a third party.[29]

As Marx's co-author and collaborator, Engels went on to be one of the most influential writers in history. He advocated "free love," the destruction of the family, and the rise of an all-embracing socialism.[30]

Enter Darwin

In 1859, Charles Darwin published *On the Origin of Species*. Ironically, although it would appear to militate against natural equality among men, Darwin's theory of evolution hastened the rise of socialism because it undermined man's belief in the Bible as

God's inspired Word. Darwin's reliance on "natural selection" helped usher in materialism, the belief that only the physical elements, as perceived by man's five senses, are real — or really matter. This fit the new doctrine of Marxism, in which man's soul was subordinated to strictly material economic concerns.

Marx himself told his colleague Engels that "Darwin's book is very important and serves me as a basis in natural science for the class struggle in history."[31]

In 1871, Darwin published *Descent of Man and Selection in Relation to Sex*, which applied the law of natural selection to human beings, suggesting an ancestry that included apes. One set of scholars summarized the impact:

> This hypothesis led to soul-searching struggles by earnest men endeavoring to reconcile traditional religious and philosophical doctrines with the new scientific tenets. Absolute values and standards were bound to be shaken.[32]

The theory of evolution also helped fuel the Nazi vision of racial supremacy as a matter of "survival of the fittest," a term invented by philosopher Herbert Spencer (1820-1903), who used it in his own *Principles of Biology* (1864) after reading *Origin of Species*.

In Germany, Adolf Hitler (1889-1945) wedded the new science of evolution with philosopher Friedrich Nietzsche's vision of the

Charles Darwin
(University College London)

"Death of God," the rise of the "Superman," and a forthcoming Master Race. While Hitler had a white-hot hatred of Jews and sought their extinction, he was also contemptuous of Christianity as a bastard offspring of Judaism. Instead of the Bible, Hitler drew his worldview from earlier, occult Aryan pagan religions.[33] He was fascinated by Nietzsche (1844-1900), as William Shirer, author of *The Rise and the Fall of the Third Reich*, observed:

> A Nazi could proudly quote [Nietzsche] on almost every conceivable subject, and did. On Christianity: "the one great curse, the one enormous and innermost perversion ... I call it the one immortal blemish of mankind...."[34]

Nietzsche eventually went mad and died in an insane asylum. But Hitler was undeterred in his admiration.

> Hitler often visited the Nietzsche museum in Weimar and publicized his veneration for the philosopher by posing for photographs of himself staring in rapture at the bust of the great man.[35]

As the first among Supermen, Hitler established himself as a god-like figure, replacing Jesus Christ in what had been a predominantly Christian country. Hitler's propaganda minister, Josef Goebbels, ordered children to recite this perverse version of the Lord's Prayer:

Adolf Hitler, you are our great leader. Thy name makes the enemy tremble. Thy Reich comes, thy will alone is law upon the Earth. Let us hear daily thy voice and order us by thy leadership, for we will obey to the end even with our lives. We praise thee! Heil Hitler![36]

Mao's Earthly Vision

In China, the communist regime published *Quotations from Chairman Mao Tse-Tung*, which became known as the "Little Red Book." Hundreds of millions of copies were distributed, and it functioned worldwide as a virtual Bible for the communist faithful. Jesus said that with faith, one can move a mountain. Mao used similar dramatic imagery:

Mao Tse-Tung

Our God is none other than the masses of the Chinese people. If they stand up and dig together with us, why can't these two mountains be cleared away?[37]

Mao's pseudo theology extended to views of death:

All men must die, but death can vary in its significance. The ancient Chinese writer Szuma Chien said, "Though death befalls all men alike, it may be heavier than Mount Tai or lighter than a feather." To die for the people is heavier than Mount Tai, but to work for the fascists and die for the exploiters and oppressors is lighter than a feather.[38]

Mao promised no afterlife, just earthly significance based on communist accomplishments in this life. By contrast, Jesus Christ promises eternal life with Him in Heaven for those who believe.

Mao died in 1976 at age 82. Biographers have since revealed that he was an outrageously cruel and perverse tyrant even in his private life, and he killed from 60 million to 100 million people on the road to his communist paradise. Today, *The Little Red Book* sits on many shelves, while China's Christian population, estimated at more than 160 million, is growing exponentially.

The hottest book in China, one for which people still risk their lives to obtain, is the Bible, whose own words warn against the absurdity of challenging God's ultimate authority:

> The kings of the earth set themselves, and the rulers take counsel together against the Lord and His Anointed, saying, "Let us break Their bonds in pieces and cast away Their cords from us." He who sits in the heavens shall laugh; the Lord shall hold them in derision (Psalm 2: 2-4).

—Robert Knight

TRUTH 3

**Socialism and Tyranny
Go Hand in Hand**

Socialism, no matter how initially intended, always resorts to coercion. That's because it is anti-God at its core and sheds the restraints of religious teaching. As Dostoevsky famously and ruefully observed in The Brothers Karamazov, *"If there is no God, then everything is permitted."*

Socialism seizes and perverts the biblical notion of charity, turning it into an excuse to empower the state. Since it can advance only at the expense of existing institutions, and because it so violates human nature and natural human relations rooted in the family, socialism is at war with normalcy itself. Men do not naturally place the needs of strangers ahead of their own families. In fact, the Bible warns that it is a sin not to provide for one's own. Charity happens after one has done that primary duty, and it is best realized on a personal level, where the giver's sacrifice is voluntary and the giver is aware of the impact of his charity. Also, real biblical charity is done out of a desire to please God and help one's neighbor.

Thomas Jefferson, American Founding Father and the author of the Declaration of Independence, de-

Thomas Jefferson
(Library of Congress)

that tax most, or 100 percent of people's income, which people naturally resent.

clared open hostility to socialism's underlying premise:

> To take from one, because it is thought his own industry and that of his fathers has acquired too much, in order to spare to others, who, or whose fathers, have not exercised equal industry and skill, is to violate arbitrarily the first principle of association, the guarantee to everyone the free exercise of his industry and the fruits acquired by it.[39]

Robbing Peter to Pay Paul

Socialism, while masquerading as a sort of compassionate mega-charity, is really a confiscatory system that ultimately requires force. Peter is robbed to pay Paul. This ensures the support of a growing number of Pauls, who develop an entitlement attitude and dependence mentality. It also ensures that the Peters are disconnected from the supposed charity done in their name with their hard-earned income. This breeds indifference to genuine suffering, since it is assumed that the government will take care of everyone's needs.

A few years ago, humorist P.J. O'Rourke facetiously introduced the "Shoot Mama" method of evaluating proposed government programs:

> All tax revenue is the result of holding a gun to somebody's head. Not paying taxes is against the law. If you don't pay your taxes, you'll be fined. If you don't pay the fine, you'll be jailed. If you try to escape from jail, you'll be shot. Thus, I — in my role as citizen and voter — am going to shoot you — in your role as taxpayer — if you don't pay your share of the national tab. Therefore, every time the government spends money on anything, you have to ask yourself, "Would I kill my kindly, gray-haired mother for this?"[40]

Humor aside, every government transfer of income involves coercion and taxation. Socialist countries are those that tax most, or 100 percent of people's income, which people naturally resent. One definition of slavery is 100 percent taxation of one's labors. So the authorities crush resistance with officially sanctioned discrimination, then persecution, and then violence.

This chilling pattern was evident in the rise of Nazi Germany, the Soviet Union, Communist China, Cuba, Cambodia, North Korea and other totalitarian nations that resorted quickly to torture and mass murder.

In 2016, it is stunning that Americans would even consider voting for an avowed socialist for president. They would certainly need to have short memories or perhaps no memory at all of the history of socialism and communism worldwide. Bernie Sanders, a Democratic candidate for president, calls himself a "democratic socialist," which by definition means state ownership of the means of production but "democratic choice over political leadership." Sanders wants to follow the models of Sweden and Norway and make all our social services "free."[41] But by-and-large people in those countries don't demonize the rich as he does.[42] Sanders would complete the redistribution of wealth that Obama began.

Bernie Sanders

In a remarkable 1985 essay about freedom, Joseph Sobran rips the "compassionate" mask off socialism:

> Nothing is more obviously characteristic of the socialist impulse than the desire to redistribute wealth. However, the end — "social justice" — is less important than the means — the power to control an entire economy.
>
> In its raw, wholesale form, socialism confiscates outright. Land is seized, major landowners are shot, farming is collectivized under state supervision. The produce is taken by the state, which unilaterally sets farm workers' wages at a considerable profit to itself. Since there are no competing employers to bid for the workers' services, the workers have no choice but to accept what they are given. This is, of course, enslavement.
>
> Trotsky appreciated this practical advantage of socialism. When the state is the sole employer, he remarked, disobedience means death by slow starvation. The Soviet Union actually starved about seven million Ukrainian farmers during the early thirties in order to implement what Stalin blandly called his "collective-farm policy" against recalcitrant elements.

Those who seek power have a natural interest in creating dependency on themselves. Where limited government and the rule of law prevail, politicians can do this only to a limited extent, through appointments and a certain amount of patronage. In this regard, socialism has opened new vistas: where the state can command a whole economy, it can make millions dependent on it for life itself. It is in this sense that socialism "works," and the socialist ruler isn't necessarily inconvenienced by the scarcity the system causes: the more desperate the people, the more they are at his mercy.[43]

From 1961 until 1989, when the Berlin Wall came down, East German guards were empowered to shoot anyone trying to leave the people's "paradise" and escape into West Germany. The same was true for all the other communist nations.

"Measures of Severity"

Many socialists deny that tyranny will eventually ensue, once their goals are met. But some freely acknowledge the need for coercion. Robert Heilbroner, an outspoken socialist and author of a number of books, including economic textbooks used in American universities, is one of the latter.

Vladimir Lenin

In 1969, he wrote:

> The real resistance to development comes
> not from the old regimes, which can be
> quickly overcome, but from the masses of the
> population who must be wrenched from their
> established ways, pushed, prodded, cajoled,
> or threatened into heroic efforts, and then
> systematically denied an increase in well-
> being so that capital can be amassed for
> future growth. This painful reorientation of a
> whole culture, judging by past experience,
> will be difficult or impossible to attain without

measures of severity.... Some nations, unfortunate in their resource endowment or in their political connections with the industrialized nations, may be forced to undergo a more or less thorough-going totalitarian transition. In general, however, when we seek to project the problems of socialism in the underdeveloped areas, we cannot sidestep the probability that intellectual stiflement, political repression, and enforced social conformity will figure prominently among them.[44]

Heilbroner's analysis dovetails with that of Vladimir Ilyich Lenin (1870-1924), communist Russia's first dictator, who boldly laid out what was necessary for the socialist transformation of society into communism:

It will be necessary under the dictatorship of the proletariat to re-educate millions of peasants and small proprietors, hundreds of thousands of office employees, officials and bourgeois intellectuals, to subordinate them all to the proletarian state and to proletarian leadership, to overcome their bourgeois habits and traditions.[45]

Joseph Stalin
(Library of Congress)

Taking this to heart, Lenin's successor, Joseph Stalin (1879-1953) ruthlessly eradicated opposition with mass murder, torture, imprisonment, confiscation of property, and persecution of Christians and other religious groups. Historian Robert Conquest estimates that Stalin killed 10 to 15 million people alone in the Ukraine by creating the great famine of 1932-1933 and dispatching people to the growing Gulag (prison system) in order to collectivize farms.[46]

In China, Mao Tse-tung (1893-1976) pursued a similarly tyrannical slaughter, saying famously,

Every Communist must grasp the truth, "Political power grows out of the barrel of a gun."[47]

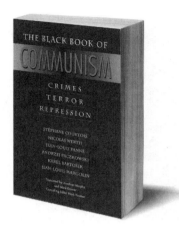

In 1999, several authors compiled *The Black Book of Communism: Crimes, Terror, Repression*, which painstakingly details the bloody cost of the worldwide experiment in the most extreme form of socialism. Their estimate: 100 million people killed.[48]

If you combine this with the millions of Jews and others killed by the Nazis, you have an unmistakably grim total of upwards of 110 million for end-game socialism in just the twentieth century.

—Robert Knight

TRUTH 4

Socialism Violates God's Law

During his campaign for president, Barack Obama invoked holy writ to answer the charge that his desire to "spread the wealth around" showed him to be a socialist. According to candidate Obama:

> My Bible tells me there is nothing wrong with helping other people. That we want to treat others like we want to be treated. That I am my brother's keeper, and I am my sister's keeper. I believe that.[49]

But the claim that Scripture sides with socialism was dismissed more than a hundred years earlier by none other than Friedrich Engels, co-author with Karl Marx of *The Communist Manifesto*, one of the world's most influential political tracts. Engels believed that "…if some few passages of the Bible may be favourable to Communism, the general spirit of its doctrines is, nevertheless, totally opposed to it…."[50]

Engels came to his conclusion honestly. Not only was he raised in a devout Christian home (from which he rebelled as a young man), he also faced opposition from at least one powerful Victorian-era minister. Author David Aikman recounts that Engels, when asked whom he hated most, gave a terse one-word answer: "Spurgeon." Engels loathed English Baptist preacher Charles Spurgeon, Aikman writes, because his

Friedrich Engels
(Newscom)

sermons reached as many as 20,000 people at a time and were "diverting England's urban working class away from atheist revolutionary socialism to Christian parliamentary reformism."[51]

Christian Socialism Not in Scripture

Despite the joint testimony of Engels and Spurgeon that Scripture is no friend to socialist thought, some Christians still think it has a biblical basis. They point to the early church in Jerusalem which, at first glance, seems like a model socialist community. The author of Acts reports that these first believers "had all things in common" (Acts 4:32) and "all who were possessors of lands or houses sold them, and brought the proceeds of the things that were sold, and laid them at the apostles' feet; and they distributed to each as anyone had need" (Acts 4:34-35).

But unlike socialism, the sharing was voluntary, not coerced. When Ananias sold some land and gave just a portion to the church, keeping the rest for himself, Peter confronted him over his lie, not his failure to give all:

> Ananias, why has Satan filled your heart to lie to the Holy Spirit and keep back part of the price of the land for yourself? While it remained, was it not your own? And after it was sold, was it not in your own control? (Acts 5:3-4).

Peter made it very clear that Ananias had every right both to own the property and to dispose of income from its sale as he wished. What he could *not* do was lie to God.

Peter acknowledged and honored the right of private ownership, but socialism does the opposite. It is a system that in both theory and practice assaults and undermines the rights of property. More than that, in almost every other way, it is at odds with the standards of God's Word.

In their *Communist Manifesto*, Marx and Engels put the "abolition of property" first in a ten-step program for implementing communism. The next three items on their list were also aimed at achieving what the authors called "despotic inroads on the rights of property":

The Death of Ananias
(Gustave Dore)

- A heavy progressive or graduated income tax.
- Abolition of all rights of inheritance.
- Confiscation of the property of all emigrants and rebels.[52]

Lenin closely followed the Marx and Engels blueprint in bringing communism to Russia. The 1918 Soviet Constitution declared that

> all private property in land is abolished, and the entire land is declared to be national property and is to be apportioned among agriculturists without any compensation to the former owners, in the measure of each one's ability to till it.[53]

While Lenin beat a hasty partial retreat four years later, due to the disastrous results of his draconian plan, the assault on property remains a defining feature of socialism wherever it is imposed. Webster's Dictionary narrowly defines socialism as "a system … in which there is no private property."[54] However, as Frederic Bastiat (1801-1850) pointed out in writing about the socialists in France in his day, it could also be called a form of "legalized" theft that can be carried out in an infinite number of ways, including "tariffs, protection, benefits, subsidies, encouragements, progressive taxation, public schools, guaranteed jobs, guaranteed profits, minimum wages, a right to relief, a right to the tools of labor, free credit, and so on…."[55]

No Exemption for Caesar

And while socialist leaders don't think so, the eighth commandment does not exempt the state. "You shall not steal" applies every bit as much to the men and women who hold the reins of political power as it does to everyone else. When Israel's King Ahab used intrigue and deceit to kill Naboth and steal his vineyard from him, God sent the prophet Elijah to deliver a severe judgment:

> You shall speak to him, saying, "Thus says the Lord: 'Have you murdered and also taken possession?'" And you shall speak to him, saying, "Thus says the Lord: 'In the place where dogs licked the blood of Naboth, dogs shall lick your blood, even yours'" (1 Kings 21:19).

God stepped in to avenge Naboth not just for his murder, but also for the theft of his property. Throughout Scripture, the sanctity of private ownership is assumed and protected. For example, the law of Moses forbids altering a neighbor's property line to encroach or usurp his land: "Cursed is the one who moves his neighbor's landmark." Author Joel McDurmon points out that other Scriptures deliver the same message, including Deuteronomy 19:14, 27:17; Job 24:2; Proverbs 22:28, 23:10; and Hosea 5:10.[56]

Dr. Calvin Beisner highlights Old Testament teaching on property with a series of rhetorical questions:

> Why does Scripture require restitution, including multiple restitution, in cases of theft, even if paying the restitution requires selling oneself into slavery (Exodus 22:1ff)? Why does God's Law specifically permit the use of force — even lethal force — to protect private property in case of a break-in at night (Exodus 22:2, 3)? And why does God's Law require showing respect for others' property by returning lost animals and helping overburdened animals, even if they belong to enemies (Exodus 23:4f)?[57]

In the New Testament, Paul writes, "Let him who stole steal no longer, but rather let him labor, working with his hands what is good, that he may have something to give him who has need" (Ephesians 4:28).

The case for Christian socialism further erodes because it is fueled in large part by envy, as chapter five reveals. The tenth commandment tell us "You shall not covet … anything that is your neighbor's" (Exodus 20:17), but Marxism, as Jewish commentator Joseph Epstein notes, is "based largely on envy." It asserts that economic inequality is a problem to be solved through the "forcible overthrow of all existing social conditions,"[58] including the "bourgeois supremacy."[59]

Seeking to Play God

Not only does socialism violate the eighth and tenth command-ments against theft and envy, it also violates the first command-ment, "You shall have no other gods before Me" (Exodus 20:3). Socialism seeks to play God, to take His place as the ultimate sovereign. It aims, like Lucifer, to "ascend into heaven," to "exalt my throne above the stars of God" (Isaiah 14:13). The state, under socialism, becomes an object of worship — not the true God.

That may sound overblown, but consider the veneration Rus-sians once gave to the embalmed remains of Lenin and Stalin. Likewise, the millions of Mao-jacket wearing Chinese, all with their copy of Chairman Mao's "Little Red Book" and the Nazi-prescribed prayer to Hitler ("Thy Reich comes, thy will alone is law upon the earth") show how socialism and its standard-bearers became idols for worship.

"Outside of socialism," said Lenin, "there is no salvation for mankind from war, hunger and the further destruction of millions and millions of human beings."[60] Twentieth century history forcefully repudiates that claim. So does Scripture. Isaiah writes, "For the LORD is our Judge, The LORD is our Lawgiver, The LORD is our King; He will save us" (Isaiah 33:22). Peter, speaking of Jesus, said, "Nor is there salvation in any other, for there is no other name under heaven given among men by which we must be saved" (Acts 4:12).

The sixth commandment, "You shall not murder," is also widely ignored by Marxist regimes to the horror and demise of millions. Marx and Engels proclaimed that their aims could be "attained only by the forcible overthrow of all existing social conditions." *The Black Book of Communism* puts the death toll from Lenin, Stalin, Mao, Pol Pot, and other communist henchmen at 100 million people. It is a "tragedy of planetary dimensions," as the French publisher of *The Black Book of Communism* put it.[61]

The killing began with Lenin, who counseled harsh means to expedite the transition from capitalism to socialism — to "purge the land of Russia of all vermin, of fleas — the rogues, of bugs — the rich, and so on and so forth." Lenin's favored techniques included imprisonment, forced labor, and terror: "one out of every ten idlers will be shot on the spot."[62]

"Little Red Book" of Chairman Mao

Heaven on Earth

A final indictment against socialism is its secularizing impact on those who live under its grip. Socialism denies the transcendent and makes material existence a matter of ultimate concern. Nineteenth century communist Moses Hess said, "The Christian … imagines the better future of the human species … in the image of heavenly joy…. We, on the other hand, will have this heaven on earth."[63]

That socialist faith turns many away from God, as Dr. D. James Kennedy noted with great insight:

> The socialist says that this is all the life there is. You only go around once; therefore, the things in this life are the only things that count, and no one must be allowed to fail. This is the only life there is, and to fail here is to fail ultimately and totally and finally and forever. The Christian says that this is a probation that is going to lead to everlasting life in heaven or hell. How we exercise this probation is going to determine what happens to us there. Therefore, every person must have an opportunity to succeed or fail. The socialist totally denies this because of his materialistic and atheistic view of life. He hinders God's purpose for life and destroys all meaning and significance.[64]

—John Aman

*An estimated 1.7 million Cambodians were killed by the communist
Khmer Rouge under Pol Pot between 1975-1979.*
(Dang Ngo/ZUMA Press)

TRUTH 5

**Envy Is the Driving
Engine of Socialism**

"Personal happiness," according to today's social scientists, is impacted more by your *"relative income disparity"* than by your own *"absolute increase in wealth."*[65] In other words, your neighbor's wealth impacts your personal happiness more than your own.

More than 200 years ago, the German philosopher Immanuel Kant had already come to the same conclusion. In defining envy, he stated:

> [I]t is a reluctance to see our own well-being overshadowed by another's because the standard we use to see how well off we are is not the intrinsic worth of our own well-being, but how it compares with that of others.[66]

Immanuel Kant

Kant saw a destructive element to envy as well: "[Envy] aims, at least in terms of one's wishes, at destroying others' good fortune."[67]

Identified as one of the "seven deadly sins," envy's destructive nature has been noted by others. Dorothy Sayers, who translated Dante's *Inferno*, where pride and envy were punished in the lower part of hell, called envy "the great leveler." She said, ". . . at its worst it is a destroyer — rather than have anyone happier than itself, it will see us all miserable together."[68]

Alexis de Tocqueville rightly recognized that "democratic institutions develop the sentiment of envy in the human heart to a very high degree" because they "awaken and flatter the passion for equality without ever being able to satisfy it entirely."[69]

Joseph Epstein, author and former editor of *The American Scholar*, considers envy one of the "cold blooded" deadly sins, emanating from a state of mind, rather than from the emotions. Envy might indeed be the cruelest sin of all, he says.[70] Epstein also sees a connection between Marxism and envy. "When I say that Marxism is based on envy, I mean that the glorious revolution of the proletariat that it promised was really a promise to put a final end to all the conditions that make for envy." He elaborates,

> The great class struggle is about nothing less than the enviable advantages that the upper classes have over the lower — advantages that, even at the cost of bloody revolution, must be eliminated. For this reason Marxism has even been described as a blood cult, with envy its abiding stimulant, fuel, and motive.[71]

Ronald Reagan
(American Vision)

Capitalist Greed vs. Socialist Envy

President Reagan called the theory of social and class warfare "alien and discredited."[72] He asked:

> Since when do we in America believe that our society is made up of two diametrically opposed classes — one rich, one poor — both in a permanent state of conflict and neither able to get ahead except at the expenses of the other?[73]

We might well ask the same question, for American politics today is rife with the politics of envy. Tommy Newberry, author of *The War on Success,* says President Obama *"stokes* envy, especially class envy."

> In Obama's eyes, America is divided between the evil rich and the virtuous exploited, and the only solution is to take from the former group and give to the latter. In fact, Obama demonizes not only the "rich," but the very act of engaging in business and making money. For him, financial success is a dishonorable goal — perversely, money is something to be taken from others, not to be earned for oneself.[74]

As Hoover Institution policy analysts Jeffrey Jones and Daniel Heil point out, traditional moral values are being turned on their head. "Previous generations thought of envious people as morally deficient; the modern world thinks the enviable are morally deficient."[75]

Surprisingly, many Christians, including both Catholics and Evangelicals, are more inclined to speak about the sin of "greed," which they associate with capitalism, than to point out the politics of envy that is pervasive in leftist and socialist propaganda.

For Christians like this, capitalism is supposed to be un-Christian or anti-Christian because it allegedly gives a predominant place to greed and other un-Christian values. It is alleged to increase poverty and the misery of the poor while, at the same time, it makes a few people rich at the expense of the many. Socialism, on the other hand, is portrayed as the economic system of people who really care for the less fortunate members of society.[76]

However, this view is based on a misunderstanding of basic principles of economics, says Dr. Jay Richards. Christians have accepted eight myths about capitalism, he says. "I'm intimately familiar with them, since they distorted my own thinking at one time."[77] One of these myths says Richards, is the belief that economics is a "zero sum game," and therefore, for someone to become rich, someone else must become poor. To the contrary, free trade increases the economic value of the goods held by all and, in fact, as the number of trading partners increases, economic value increases at an exponential, not an incremental, rate.

Purveyors of the Politics of Envy
Indeed, when free trade and free enterprise are operative, there is little temptation to envy. As syndicated columnist Paul Greenberg wrote in 2007,

> Are we really supposed to be unhappy because somewhere in this country others are richer or happier than we are? . . . Americans are basically a forward-looking, enterprising and confident lot who aren't much for envying the rich. Especially since we hope to join them someday.[78]

But that was written before then-Sen. Barack Obama had won the election.

> . . . [O]n the eve of Martin Luther King Jr. Day, the incoming president stood at the civil rights leader's historic pulpit and spoke of the need for unity. Americans must unite, Obama demanded, to end the country's moral deficit.

> "CEOs are making more in ten minutes than some workers make in ten months," he said. In an interview with *The New York Times* a few weeks later, Obama criticized the "structural imbalance in our economy . . . where increasingly the benefits of economic growth [are] accruing to a smaller band of people."[79]

Speeches and interviews such as these have been described by Hoover policy analysts Jones and Heil, as a "crusade against income inequality." It's a crusade, they say, in which President Obama has been joined by mouthpieces of the Left, such as the self-described "flagship of the left," *The Nation* magazine, as well as the radical Institute for Policy Studies.

As Jones and Heil see it, "Reducing income inequality through redistributive policies aims to punish the 'haves' as much as it claims to help the 'have-nots.' Focusing on relative disparities suggests that people have the right to resent others' good fortune, hard work, or income."[80] But such is the politics of envy.

Subsequent actions of the Obama administration, including pay cuts for executives at all companies that received the 2008 bailout, have also played to the politics of envy, says Linda Chavez, former staff director of the U.S. Commission on Civil Rights for President Reagan. She notes how the envy is selectively expressed:

> The populist zeal to seek revenge on those who make a lot of money is targeted almost exclusively at corporations. I haven't heard outcries about Hollywood actors who make millions per film.[81]

Dr. Walter Williams

What happens when politicians pit us against these rich executives? Dr. Walter Williams, the noted economist, says, "It's a slick political sleight-of-hand where politicians and their allies amongst the intellectuals, talking heads, and the news media get us caught up in the politics of envy as part of their agenda for greater control over our lives."[82]

Redistributive policies that aim to reduce income inequality are foreign to the principles of a free market economy and voluntary exchange. Such policies become commonplace, however, in a society driven by the politics of envy.

"Spreading the Wealth" Is Legal Plunder

Our Founders recognized that, given human nature, envy could become a driving force in politics, and they designed the Constitution to protect our God-given rights, including the right to private property, from the grasping hand of a tyrannical government. But if a "loophole" can be found in the Constitution in order to justify redistribution of property, politicians can advance their socialist goals through the courts and legislatures.

President Obama doesn't call it a "loophole." He calls it a "blind spot."

> I think we can say that the Constitution reflected an enormous blind spot in this culture that carries on until this day, and the framers had that same blind spot. . . . The Supreme Court never ventured into the issues of redistribution of wealth and sort of more basic issues of political and economic justice in this society.[83]

What Obama calls a "blind spot," is really a reflection of the Founders' view of limited government and their understanding of the role of the law in society. Having taught constitutional law, Obama understands well enough, as he has said, that

> [t]he Constitution is a chart of negative liberties, [it] says what the states can't do to you, says what the federal government can't do to you, but it doesn't say what the federal government or the state government must do on your behalf.[84]

He's just not happy with this fact.

The Founders understood that the negative function of the law as organized justice is to protect our God-given rights of life, liberty, and property. They never intended for the law to assume the affirmative role of giving "rights" or "entitlements" to certain groups or individuals. Yet this view is common to socialists. Frederic Bastiat calls such use of the law *legal plunder*. When socialism was taking hold in France, Bastiat saw clearly how socialists used the law to further their ends. Writing in 1850, he said,

Under the pretense of organization, regulation, protection, or encouragement, the law takes property from one person and gives it to another; the law takes the wealth of all and gives it to a few — whether farmers, manufacturers, ship owners, artists, or comedians.[85]

In the end, it doesn't matter *who* benefits — whether it's the poor, the rich, the elderly, or the legislators themselves — it's all the same. It is *legal plunder,* says Bastiat, for the law has been the means to *take* property — plunder — from one group in order to *give* it to another.

Frederic Bastiat
(The Warren J. Samuels Portrait Collection at Duke University)

Once legal plunder through taxation and redistribution of income has been accepted by the populace as a legitimate function of government, the goal of each social group —whether it's comedians or car-makers — is to gain either legislative power for themselves or influence and access to those who have it.

This was clearly evident in September 2011 when demonstrators filled a park in New York City's Wall Street financial district, protesting income disparity between the "99 percent" and America's wealthiest one percent. Protesting college students called for free college tuition for all, a demand that socialist Bernie Sanders is now promising to fulfill if elected.

Spiritual Root of the Problem

Even some socialists are recognizing that envy is counterproductive. As one has written, "the very passions that have been mobilized against oppressive inequality shade easily into envy, envy of a particularly destructive sort."[86] Nevertheless, socialists persist in claiming that creating "a more egalitarian social order" is the key to eliminating "oppressive inequality." This will not, however, solve the problem of envy, for envy is a matter of the heart and the human heart is "deceitful above all things" (Jeremiah 17:9).

Furthermore, as Dr. D. James Kennedy has pointed out, the sinful nature of the unredeemed person has "virtually unlimited wants and desires for material things," while his ability to produce to meet these wants is severely limited. Thus, the unregenerate person "is always looking for some way other than God to meet his many wants and needs."[87]

In contrast, however, the person who has been redeemed by Jesus Christ and regenerated by the Spirit of God and has trusted in Jesus Christ for salvation, has a greatly reduced set of wants and needs. In addition, as a new creature in Christ, he has God's wisdom, help, and strength available to help meet his wants and needs. He does not worry about his needs, for he knows that God will supply them as He has promised.[88]

That is why the politics of envy should have no appeal for anyone who has trusted in Christ and experienced His saving grace.

God commands us not to covet anything that is our neighbor's. Likewise, He has much to say about envy in the book of Proverbs. "Envy is rottenness to the bones" (Proverbs 14:30), and "Do not let your heart envy sinners, but be zealous for the fear of the LORD all the day" (Proverbs 23:17).

Therefore, if envy is the "driving engine" of socialism, no Christian should get on board that train.

—Karen VanTil Gushta

TRUTH 6

**Socialism Failed at Jamestown
and Plymouth**

Call them pilot projects for socialism. Long before Jean-Jacques Rousseau spun fanciful notions about noble savages and collective ownership, the hardy Brits who settled Jamestown and Plymouth tested his ideas for him. Too bad Rousseau didn't take note.

Not only did the fierce natives encountered in Virginia and New England severely test Rousseau's happy talk about man in the state of nature, but his claim — and that of others after him — that society is best organized as a collective, where the individual and his property are placed in submission to the "General Will," was tried and found wanting. And then some.

First Jamestown and then Plymouth began with a system of common ownership dictated by investors. That quasi-socialist system quickly proved disastrous, both north and south, and had to be scrapped for another, which gave these first Americans the right to keep the fruits of their labor — and incentive to produce more.

The 104 Jamestown settlers who stepped ashore in Virginia on May 14, 1607, were entranced by what they found. Spring was in its full verdant splendor, and they found "all the ground bespread with many sweet and delicate flowers of divers colors and kinds."[89] The woods were dense with beech, oak, cedar, cypress, and walnut trees, along with strawberries, mul-

berries, raspberries, and "Fruites unknowne." Fish in abundance sported in the rivers, including sturgeon ("all the world cannot be compared to it") and they found "great store" of deer, bears, foxes, otters, beavers, and muskrats. After their long Atlantic crossing, these bedazzled English arrivals concluded that "heaven and earth never agreed better to frame a place for man's habitation."[90]

Or so they thought.

Life quickly turned very hard, as malaria, famine, and attacks by native Indians quickly took their toll. Food was in such short supply during the winter of 1609 that "famine crazed men even dogged the steps of those of their comrades who were not quite wasted, threatening to kill and devour them."[91] Just 60 of 500 settlers who had arrived in Jamestown survived.[92]

So how did they manage to starve in this land of milk and honey?

De Facto Socialism

Jamestown settlers were saddled under their charter with seven years of indentured servitude, during which time the colony's produce was held jointly. The de facto socialist system employed a common store for food and clothing, and many settlers were gentlemen unfit for and unused to physical labor. The colonists had a small plot of land to look forward to after their seven years of service, but common ownership in the interim offered little incentive, and few exerted themselves by planting crops or working in other ways to provide for their needs. Many devoted themselves to a futile attempt to hit nature's jackpot by panning for gold and looked to friendly Indians to help fill their bellies.[93]

Nineteenth century historian James Eggleston said of arrangements in Jamestown:

> Better devices for promoting indolence and aggravating the natural proneness to dissension of men in hard circumstances could scarcely have been hit upon. Anarchy and despotism are the inevitable alternatives under such a communistic arrangement, and each of these ensued in turn.[94]

The despotism came with the arrival of Sir Thomas Dale in 1611, who imposed severe discipline upon the remaining members of the Virginia Company, including requirements for religious observance and regular work. But along with the cruel and exacting rigors of his "Lawes Divine, Morall and Martiall," Dale provided the inhabitants with incentive by giving some settlers three acres of land to plant and work for their own individual benefit.

The result was striking. According to the account of one Jamestown settler, James Hamor, hunger quickly abated after the settlers were given their own land to work.

> For formerly, when our people were fed out of the common store and labored jointly in the manuring of the ground, and planting corn, glad was that man that could slip from his labor, nay the most honest of them in a general business would not take so much faithful and true pains in a week, as now he will do in a day. Neither cared they for the increase, presuming

Landing of the Pilgrims
(Architect of the Capitol)

that howsoever their harvest prospered, the general store must maintain them, by which means we reaped not so much corn from the labors of 30 men, as three men have done for themselves.[95]

It was a lesson the Pilgrims had to learn as well.

Just as in Jamestown, the 104 people who arrived at Plymouth Rock on December 21, 1620, were organized under a charter which imposed a seven-year period of joint ownership in which all the fruits of their labor were held in common. The agreement was not to the Pilgrim's liking but was required by the merchants who underwrote the colony. Thus, from the day they arrived in the new world, all clothing, houses, lands, crops, and cash were jointly owned. No matter how hard a man might work, he had little hope of personal gain for his effort. Aside from the Pilgrims' ardent Christian faith, life in Plymouth was a "worker's paradise" of which Marx and Engels would have been proud.

At Odds With Human Nature

In fact, it was a social order at odds with the dictates of human nature and resulted in what historian Eggleston termed a "sinking of personal interest …, in dissensions and insubordination, in unthrift and famine."[96]

The communal arrangement also ill-fitted the Pilgrims for life on the edge of a "howling wilderness." The first fierce New England winter took a heavy toll. The Pilgrims buried 44 people within the first three months, and a total of 50 poor wretches succumbed within the first year. The Pilgrims gathered what Governor Bradford described as a "small harvest" and celebrated their first Thanksgiving with the Indians in the autumn of 1621. Another small harvest followed in 1622. The meager return from the ground came in part because the Pilgrims were unskilled as farmers and because the sandy

Husbands "deemed it a kind of slavery" that
**their wives were conscripted to serve other men,
"dressing their meat, washing their clothes, etc."**
— Governor William Bradford

New England soil was poor. However, it was the lack of any promise of return for their labors that caused even these God-fearing and devout settlers to fail to fully work the land.

Governor Bradford wrote that the system of communal property "was found to breed much confusion and discontent, and retard much employment which would have been to the general benefit and comfort." The young men, Bradford wrote, were ill-disposed to labor on behalf of the wives and children of other men without any recompense. More seasoned and accomplished men took it as an affront to be on par and forced to share in the same labor and rations as the "meaner and younger sort." And husbands "deemed it a kind of slavery" that their wives were conscripted to serve other men, "dressing their meat, washing their clothes, etc."[97]

While fishing helped make up the shortfall from the field, the "pinch of hunger" forced the Pilgrims to abandon their corporate charter in March of 1623. After "much debate," Governor Bradford

> allowed each man to plant corn for his own particular [for his own household] and to trust themselves for that . . . so every family was assigned a parcel of land, according to the proportion of their number . . . this was very successful. It made all hands very industrious, so that much more corn was planted than otherwise would have been by any means the Governor or any other could devise.[98]

William Bradford
(American Vision)

Pilgrims' Progress

Suddenly, these heretofore mediocre farmers made their own capitalist "great leap forward." Authors D. James Kennedy and Charles Hull Wolfe report that while the Pilgrims planted 26 acres of corn, barley, and peas in 1621, and nearly 60 acres the next year, they planted 184 acres in 1623.[99]

Bradford reported that "instead of famine, now God gave them plenty, and the face of things was changed, to the rejoicing of the hearts of many, for which they blessed God." Under the new system of private enterprise, "any general want or famine hath not been amongst them since to this day."[100]

With the Indian trade, an ample food supply, and God's blessing, the Pilgrims grew in prosperity and were soon able to buy out the interest of their investors and obtain clear title to their land.[101]

For Bradford, the lesson was very clear:

The experience that was had in this common course and condition, tried sundry years and that amongst godly and sober men, may well evince the vanity of that conceit of Plato's and other ancients applauded by some of later times; that the taking away of property and bringing in community into a commonwealth would make them happy and flourishing; as if they were wiser than God.[102]

God, Bradford said, "in *His* wisdom had another course fitter for them."[103]

—John Aman

TRUTH 7

Socialism Impoverishes Nations

Acting fast and without remorse, Vladimir Lenin imposed socialism on Russia within months of the October 1917 revolution. Swept along by revolutionary fervor and the mandate of Marxism, Lenin's Bolsheviks confiscated landed estates, nationalized banks, criminalized stock and bond sales, and took control of small industrial enterprises.

It was the "closest example of full-blown theoretical socialism the world has ever seen," write economists Peter J. Boettke and Peter T. Leeson.[104] And the most disastrous.

Historian and journalist William Chamberlin commented:

> War Communism may fairly be considered one of the greatest and most overwhelming failures in history. Every branch of economic life, industry, agriculture, transportation, experienced conspicuous deterioration and fell far below the pre-War levels of output.[105]

Soviet economic output dropped to 14 percent of the pre-1917 level by 1921 and Lenin had to stage a tactical retreat with his New Economic Policy that allowed for a partial market economy to operate.[106] Capitalism was needed to salvage communism.

But that first demonstration project showing how fast socialism can devastate an economy did little to dampen enthusiasm for Marxist ideas in Russia or elsewhere.

In the case of China, it took 30 years of applied socialism and the death of millions before Chinese leaders took their first faltering steps in 1978 toward economic liberalization. At that point, the average wage was about one dollar a day.[107]

Unblemished Record
After nearly 100 years, socialism has an unblemished record of failure. Wherever central planning and state control have taken the place of private ownership and market forces, the result has been the same. A descent into poverty.

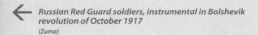

Tanzania's President Julius Nyerere declared war on poverty in 1965 and designated socialism as the means by which the struggle would be won. As president of a one-party state, he had the means to achieve his socialist solution. Over nearly 30 years in power, his government nationalized land, banks, established some 4,000 government corporations, and set prices on some 3,000 consumer goods.[108]

But even though Nyerere had nearly three decades to defeat poverty and enjoyed a windfall of financial aid from the West (and China) totaling $20 billion by one estimate, his attempt was a spectacular failure. The war on poverty was decisively lost.

Under socialism some food crops, such as maize, which were once exports, had to be imported to help feed the nation. Pastor and opposition party leader Rev. Christopher Mtikila remembers how widespread hunger prompted Nyerere to go on the radio to "tell the nation that we must tighten the belts…. [W]e should tighten the belts, then the hunger would not be felt, because the stomach has been made small."[109]

Author Joshua Muravchik explains that the economic inefficiencies imposed by Nyerere's socialist system, which Nyerere

Tanzania President Julius Nyerere, center,
with Cuban dictator Fidel Castro, left, in 1977
(Keystone Pictures/Zuma)

embraced while a student at the University of Edinburgh, included a shoe factory that operated at four percent capacity and a fertilizer company that took in 140,000 tons of imports to produce 100,000 tons of fertilizer.[110]

Muravchik cites a World Bank study that found Tanzania's economy shrunk a half percent each year, on average, from 1965-1988. Other experts, he writes, believe economic growth did not outpace population.[111]

"Let's Admit It."

Nyerere resigned the presidency in 1985, but served as chairman of the ruling political party until 1990. He summarized the outcome of his economic experiment in his presidential farewell, saying, "I failed. Let's admit it."[112]

It was not so much Nyerere, but the system he adopted that failed. The nearly 60 African or Arab Third World nations that also embraced socialism by the 1970s achieved similar results. "Scarcely any achieved robust growth," Muravchik writes, "and many suffered stagnation or even decline, although their starting points were low."[113]

The result has been the same in Latin America. Food is rationed in Cuba, and Venezuela now rations water and electricity. Oil production in Venezuela declined from 3.2 million barrels a day in 1998, when Hugo Chavez first came to power, to 2.4 million barrels a day in 2008.[114] One review of the economic performance of socialist nations in Latin American that looked at GDP, investment, inflation, employment, and exports concluded that "21st Century Socialism has failed to deliver a meaningfully improved standard of living."[115]

Sweden, sometimes seen as a socialist success story, conforms to the pattern of penury. While Sweden enjoyed a per capita income almost equal to the U.S. in the late 1960s, growth stalled after it became a cradle-to-grave socialist state. Personal tax rates of 65 to 75 percent, high business taxes, restrictive labor regulations, and government debt that ran to 71 percent of GDP by 1993, combined with other factors to bring economic growth "to a crawl," reports economist Richard Rahn.[116] The Nordic nation fell from 5th to 14th place in the Organisation for Economic Co-operation and Development "prosperity index" between 1970 and 2003.[117]

Freedom and Prosperity Linked

The Index of Economic Freedom, which ranks some 179 nations and is released annually by the Heritage Foundation, has consistently found a positive relationship between freedom and prosperity. In general, the more free an economy — the more it embraces market capitalism — the more prosperity it enjoys, as the chart nearby illustrates. The top 10 most free economies on the Index are: Hong Kong, Singapore, New Zealand, Switzerland, Australia, Canada, Chile, Ireland, Estonia, and the United

The United States economic freedom score is 75.4, making its economy the 11th freest in the 2016 Index of Economic Freedom. "Americans continue to lose economic freedom. Following declines in seven of the past eight years, the United States this year has equaled its worst score ever in the Index of Economic Freedom. Ratings for labor freedom, business freedom, and fiscal freedom have flagged notably, and the regulatory burden is increasingly costly."

— The Heritage Foundation

Kingdom. The United States is eleventh on the list. The bottom 10 feature an odd assortment of rogue, socialist, or dysfunctional states, including North Korea, Cuba, Venezuela, Zimbabwe, Turkmenistan, Eritrea, Republic of Congo, Iran, Equatorial Guinea, and Argentina. [118]

So why does socialism bring economic decline? It has to do with prices, profits, and private property. Socialism does away with the latter two and, in so doing, eliminates both the incentive to produce and the information needed for realistic prices and rational economic decisions. When government dictates prices and production quotas, and imposes stringent regulations on businesses, true thriving economic activity becomes impossible.

Without the information provided in a free market by prices and profits (losses, too), what Austrian economist Ludwig von Mises called "economic calculation" becomes impossible. With socialism, he said, "there is only groping in the dark," as central planners, deprived of the demand and scarcity signals provided by market prices, try to allocate resources, determine needs, and set prices.

Ludwig von Mises
(Ludwig von Mises Institute)

Without the feedback delivered in a free market by profits and losses, a socialist system has no gauge to measure success or failure. Economist Mark J. Perry comments,

> Without profits, there is no way to discipline firms that fail to serve the public interest and no way to reward firms that do. There is no efficient way to determine which programs should be expanded and which ones should be contracted or terminated.[119]

The distortion of economic decision making is so complete under socialism that von Mises, writing 90 years ago, called it "the abolition of rational economy."[120]

Socialism, however, does send a clear signal to investors, telling them to send their money elsewhere or put it under the mattress. Under socialism, the rate of investment quickly drops, capital formation suffers, the capital stock declines,[121] and innovation grinds to a halt.

Investment Declines Under Socialism

Writing in 1990, scholar Tom Palmer described the aging and decrepit condition of Eastern Europe after decades of socialism:

> Most of the textile mills in eastern Czechoslovakia were built before the First World War. They still operate with the original machinery.

In East Germany, many of the buildings seem not to have been painted since 1945. In some cases, no one even painted over the old and faded Nazi slogans on the walls. In the Soviet Union, there are chemical factories built 110 years ago that are still producing the same chemicals in the same way. It is a general principle that under socialism, no factory is ever closed.[122]

Without investment to build new plants and introduce more efficient technologies, living standards decline. The Venezuelan government imposed electricity rationing in 2009 in large part because of under-investment in its electricity infrastructure. While dictator Hugo Chávez blamed his nation's hydro-electric power shortage on an El Niño drought, economic analysts Daniel Wagner and C. J. Redfern suggest a lack of investment is more likely to blame:

In Venezuela, less than a quarter of the $643 million budgeted for electricity infrastructure projects between 2001 and 2005 was actually spent, and less than 10 percent of the additional electricity generating capacity deemed necessary for the country's growing population 10 years ago has been realized.[123]

The paralyzing influence of central planning also takes its toll on innovation. Economist Milton Friedman wrote in 1989 that even in the mostly free economy of the U.S., the areas most heavily controlled by the government — the post office and schools, for example — are also the ones "mired in outdated technology."[124]

When private property is displaced by a system of common ownership, there is little incentive to maintain and develop capital assets. As economist Mark Perry explains:

> While private property creates incentives for conservation and the responsible use of property, public property encourages irresponsibility and waste. If everyone owns an asset, people act as if no one owns it. And when no one owns it, no one really takes care of it. Public ownership encourages neglect and mismanagement.[125]

It's the difference between Amtrak and Southwest Airlines.

—John Aman

TRUTH 8

Socialism Is at War
With the Family

Homeschooling parents Uwe and Hannelore Romeike fled Germany in 2008 with their five children after a two-year struggle with the German state. At one point, German police forcibly removed two of the couple's five children from their home in Bissinggen and took them — crying and terrified — to school.

Moving to Tennessee, the Romeikes sought asylum from the U.S. government, and a U.S. federal judge granted their request in January 2010. His conclusion: German authorities had persecuted them for teaching their children at home. In his ruling, the immigration judge said the Romeikes' right to homeschool their children "are basic human rights that no country has a right to violate." He added, "Homeschoolers are a particular social group that the German government is trying to suppress. This

Homeschooling parents Uwe and Hannelore Romeike with three of their five children.

family has a well-founded fear of persecution … therefore, they are eligible for asylum … and the court will grant asylum."[126]

According to the family's attorney, Michael Donnelly, parents in Germany can face fines, loss of custody, and even jail, if they want to homeschool their children. Parents can send their children to private schools, but the curriculum is still state approved, and parents have no means of protecting their children from teachings they deem harmful.

Although compulsory education in Germany predated Adolf Hitler's rise to power, the present laws were set in place during Hitler's efforts to indoctrinate the nation's youth into his ideas of National Socialism. Hitler was adamant that "this new Reich will give its youth to no one, but will itself take youth and give to youth its own education and its own upbringing."[127]

As Michael Donnelly observes, "If you want to control the culture, you need to control the children and what they think, and how they're taught."[128] But the socialist agenda is broader than simply controlling children. In his book, *Fighting for America's Soul,* Robert Knight explains why socialism has always been bad for families.

> Socialism has been at war with the family since becoming a political and philosophical force in the nineteenth century. Man's natural inclination is to provide for himself and his own family, then his neighbors and community. Socialism must remove such existing

Nazi poster reads: "Youth serves the leader.
All ten year-olds into the Hitler Youth."
(Library of Congress)

loyalties and institutions in order to replace them with government power. That's why socialists have been a major force behind the sexual revolution of abortion, homosexuality, and pornography, because all these things hurt the family. As families crumble, the state steps in to take their place.[129]

An Army of Young Radicals

Taking away the biblical prerogative of parents to educate their own children and indoctrinating youth into socialism are ways socialists gain control in a society. As Dr. Erwin Lutzer points out in *When a Nation Forgets God,*

Hitler's educational philosophy was patterned after that of the Soviet revolutionaries. His goal was to build an army of young radicals who would pay lip service to the past but forge a new path that would ensure that German ideals were passed on from generation to generation.[130]

Every socialist crusade since the Russian Bolsheviks has tried to build an "army of young radicals." Therefore, it should come as no surprise that the 20th century neo-Marxists saw their opportunity to enlist rebellious college students of the 1960s in their efforts to subvert American culture. As historian William S. Lind explains:

A whole generation of Americans, especially the university-educated elite, absorbed cultural Marxism as their own, accepting a poisonous ideology that sought to destroy America's traditional culture and Christian faith. That generation, which runs every elite institution in America, now wages a ceaseless war on all traditional beliefs and institutions.[131]

The ideology of "radical equality," which has become dominant on college campuses across America has brought its inevitable consequence—totalitarianism and tyranny. "Thought police" are quick to sue anyone who dares cross the lines set by gender feminists, homosexual activists, or local black or Hispanic groups. Political correctness rules. [132]

The downstream effects of the takeover of higher education by cultural Marxists are now evident in the infatuation of America's youth with a socialist running for the presidency. When Bernie Sanders beat Hillary Clinton in the New Hampshire democratic primary by 84 to 15 percent among voters under 30, it became clear who was listening to his message and liking it. [133]

Sexual Promiscuity — the Socialist's Tool

Besides their efforts to indoctrinate America's youth by teaching at universities and propagandizing for far-left politics, another way socialists radicalize youth is by encouraging them to become sexually promiscuous. Socialists are forthright in claiming their goal is to "not only end economic exploitation, but also bring about personal and sexual freedom." The Russian Revolution of 1917 brought in a period of sexual freedom, which Stalin later crushed after consolidating power. During this early period, sex between men was decriminalized, abortion was legalized, along with homosexual marriage, and divorce was available upon request.[134]

Likewise, when 98 percent of Austrians voted to come under German rule in 1938, drastic changes soon followed. On the day of the election, March 13, crucifixes were taken down from the nation's classrooms and replaced with a Nazi flag and a picture of Adolf Hitler. Kitty Werthmann, whose mother sent her to a convent to protect her from the upheaval, recounts,

> Every once in a while, on holidays, I went home. I would go back to my old friends and ask what was going on and what they were doing. Their loose lifestyle was very alarming to me. They lived without religion. By that time unwed mothers were glorified for having a baby for Hitler. It seemed strange to me that our society changed so suddenly.[135]

Werthmann now speaks around the country about her experiences.

> When the mothers had to go out into the work force, the government immediately established child care centers. You could take your children, ages four weeks to school age, and leave them there around-the-clock, seven days a week, under the total care of the government. The state raised a whole generation of children.[136]

Sex Education Incites Sexual Activity

"Sex education in the schools appears to operate more as an incitement to sexual activity than as a heeded caution…. [T]he message that the students are expected to engage in sex is always there," says Judge Robert Bork in his book, *Slouching Towards Gomorrah*.[137] His observation has been confirmed by a recent report which showed that teens exposed to so-called safe-sex programs engaged in more sexual activity than the control group, who received neither a "safe sex" nor an abstinence message. By contrast, two years after learning about abstinence, two-thirds of the students had not become sexually active.[138]

The evidence is growing that abstinence education is, in fact, the only effective way to curb rising pregnancy rates among youth. Yet the Obama administration cut funding for these programs, leaving schools to teach only the condom-based "safe sex" approach — the approach favored by most sex education programs across the country.

Dr. Miriam Grossman warns parents to beware of such sex education programs, stating flatly, "the people teaching your child are activists, promoting radical agendas at odds with your values."[139] Rooted in the warped thinking of the late sex researcher Alfred C. Kinsey, such groups as the Sexuality Information and Education Council of the United States (SIECUS), Planned Parenthood, and Advocates for Youth want to integrate sex education "across the curriculum," and the earlier the better. Their goal is to indoctrinate children with the view that sexuality is "who they are" and "anything goes" when it comes to sexual experience. Furthermore, parents should support their children in their quest to "develop their own values."[140]

Simply put, sex education materials from SIECUS and Planned Parenthood promote promiscuity. As Frank York and Jan LaRue write in *Protecting Your Child in an X-Rated World*, "SIECUS is firmly committed to promoting unrestrained sexual activities for children."[141] The founder of SIECUS, Mary Calderone, was the medical director of Planned Parenthood and supported such ideas as "child sexuality," merging or reversing the sexes or sex roles, liberating children from their families, and abolishing the family as we know it.[142]

SIECUS is not alone in its efforts. The United Nations Population Fund (UNFPA) and the UN Educational, Scientific and Cultural Organization (UNESCO) have co-sponsored a curriculum that

Dr. Mary Calderone (1965)
(Library of Congress)

includes "teaching children as young as five to be sexually active and training adolescents to advocate for abortion."[143] When the 54th session of the UN Commission on the Status of Women (CSW) was held at the UN in March 2010, the World Association of Girl Scouts and Girl Guides hosted a "no-adults-welcome" panel for teen girls. A brochure entitled "Healthy, Happy and Hot" turned up among the materials available to the teenage girls attending.[144] The pamphlet, produced by the International Planned Parenthood Federation, gushed, "[T]here are lots of different ways to have sex and lots of different types of sex. There is no right or wrong way to have sex. Just have fun, explore, and be yourself!"[145]

Redefining the Family Structure

Along with teaching that "anything goes" when it comes to sexual behavior, youth are being taught new definitions of the family, such as "a unit of two or more persons, related either by birth or by choice, who may or may not live together, who try to meet each others needs and share common goals and interests."[146] Since *Stone v. Graham* (1980), America's government controlled schools have not been allowed to post the Ten Commandments, lest children "read, meditate upon, perhaps ... venerate and obey" them.[147] Now they are forsaking traditional morality and biblical definitions of the family.

Irving Kristol, an early voice for American neoconservatism, wrote that "even moderate socialist movements and governments" are hostile to the family, although this hostility is "often cloaked as indifference." Kristol saw evidence of this hostility among liberals as well. "All liberal politicians today speak highly of the family . . . but they cannot bring themselves to defend it against its enemies." According to Kristol, these enemies include radical feminists and homosexual activists.[148]

Feminists and homosexual militants are just following the agenda laid down by Marx and Engels, who wanted to abolish the "bourgeois" family along with private property. "On what foundation is the present family, the bourgeois family, based?" they wrote, "On capital, on private gain. In its completely developed form, this family exists only among the bourgeoisie.... The bourgeois family will vanish as a matter of course when its complement [prostitution among the proletariat class] vanishes, and both will vanish with the vanishing of capital."[149]

For decades, liberals, progressives, and socialists in America have been promoting public policies that lead to greater promiscuity, illegitimate births, abortions, and unwed mothers. This is no accident, as Dr. Allan Carlson of the Howard Center for Family, Religion, and Society points out:

> Healthy and stable families are essential to the preservation of a free society. They limit the size and intrusiveness of government, promote public engagement, stabilize neighborhoods, and build the institutions of civil society.[150]

Healthy and stable families are the fountain of culture and society. [151] However, America's families are under attack from socialists and progressives. Policies of the so-called Great Society undermined the strength of the black family unit, and same-sex "marriage" introduced the notion that healthy families need not include both a father and a mother. [152]

Recent research also shows that most Americans do not include "family" as a primary cultural value. Compared to many South Asian societies that rank "family" at the top of the list, North Americans rank "religion" first, followed by "individualism, risk-taking, self-reliance, and equity."[153] Yet, clearly, "religion" that fails to follow God's plan for the family will neither bring revival to America nor advance the kingdom of God.

Our concern over the efforts of socialists to undermine the strength of our families should not prompt us to hunker down in Christian cultural bunkers in order to protect our children. We cannot idolize our families. More than ever, Christians need to be in the forefront of society, proclaiming God's Gospel for all of life and showing how His divine design gives each sphere of society its rightful place and ruling authority, and how the Christian family is, indeed, the wellspring of a healthy society.

—Karen VanTil Gushta

TRUTH 9

Socialism Is at War
With the Church

I beg you; look for the words "social justice" or "economic justice" on your church web site. If you find it, run as fast as you can. Social justice and economic justice, they are code words.[154]

So said television social commentator Glenn Beck on his program on March 2, 2010.

Beck's comments provoked immediate response from Jim Wallis, president of *Sojourners*. "What he has said attacks the very heart of our Christian faith, and Christians should no longer watch his show," Wallis said.[155]

It is no surprise that Wallis would be the first to respond to Beck. The *Sojourners* website is self-described as "a progressive Christian commentary on faith, politics, and culture."[156] The mission of *Sojourners* is "to articulate the biblical call to social justice, inspiring hope and building a movement to transform individuals, communities, the church, and the world."[157]

Should Christians be getting behind *Sojourners* and stop listening to Glenn Beck?

Glenn Beck
(Gage Skidmore)

Dr. D. James Kennedy pointed out in his sermon, "The Bible and Economics":

> Confusing justice and charity has produced something called "social justice," the basis for the welfare state. . . . Behind this notion of social justice is the idea that there must be a more equitable distribution of wealth.[158]

Christian Charity or Government Welfare?

Despite the efforts of Charles Haddon Spurgeon and others, such as the great nineteenth century American theologian Charles Hodge,[159] to unmask socialism's true face during their lifetimes, Christians have flirted with it for the past 150 years. Even today the notion that Christians should support government efforts to redistribute private property under the banner of "social justice" appeals to many. They argue that Jesus' concern for the poor justifies supporting government social welfare programs.

Charles Spurgeon
(Newscom)

The genuine concern that Christians should have for those in need and the blessings that follow from exercising Christian charity are subverted, however, when we turn over this responsibility to government agencies. As Dr. Kennedy noted in a sermon, "Does the Bible Teach Socialism?"

> One thing we ought to clearly understand — you will attain no moral or spiritual merit from giving that is coerced. . . . If there is no motivation of voluntary giving, there is no spiritual aspect to the deed.[160]

If you are forced to give to your government in order to "spread the wealth," you are not going to receive any rewards in heaven for "giving a cup of water" in Jesus' name. Governments do not give in the name of Jesus. They give in their own name, and the politicians who pass the entitlement legislation to "redistribute the wealth" get the "glory."

Nevertheless, so-called Liberation Theology has made inroads among many clergy, not the least notable being President Obama's former pastor, Jeremiah Wright. As Robert Knight writes in *Radical Rulers: The White House Elites Who are Pushing America Toward Socialism,* "For 20 years Obama sat in the pews with his family and listened to Wright preach radical, race-centered Marxism dressed up in Christian clothing. . . . [H]is main theme is black liberation theology."[161]

Acton Research Institute Fellow Anthony B. Bradley looked closely at Wright's views and described them this way:

> Among all of [the] controversial comments by Jeremiah Wright, the idea of massive wealth redistribution is the most alarming.... Black Liberation theologians have explicitly stated a preference for Marxism as an ethical framework for the black church because Marxist thought is predicated on a system of oppressor class (whites) versus victim class (blacks).[162]

Bradley notes that thinkers such as James Cone and Cornel West have been working since the 1970s to "embed Marxist thought into the black church." According to James Cone, "… the Christian faith does not possess in its nature the means for analyzing the structure of capitalism. Marxism as a tool of social analysis can disclose the gap between appearance and reality and thereby help Christians to see how things really are."[163]

Using the Bible to Promote Socialism

Using biblical references to promote socialism is a common ploy of American socialists, says author Tommy Newberry in his book *The War on Success*.

> After all, our nation was founded on biblical principles, and according to recent polls, 80 percent of Americans claim to believe in God,

Rev. Jeremiah Wright Jr.
(Zuma)

and 77 percent profess to be either Christian or Jewish. Socialists can't explicitly reject God and expect to win election, so instead they try to co-opt Him as a salesman for their atheistic cause.[164]

While some use biblical allusions and quotes to promote socialist ideas, and some claim the church should use Marxism as a "tool of social analysis," a growing number within the church are attempting "to use the Bible as a weapon against capitalism."[165]

In his book, *Poverty and Wealth: Why Socialism Doesn't Work,* Ronald H. Nash points out that liberal Protestants attacked principles of economic freedom in the 1930s and '40s. But now such radical views are popping up even among evangelical

Karl Marx praised the Communards
of the French Revolution who boasted,

"Our enemy is God. Hatred of God is the beginning of wisdom."

Christians who are "recommending socialism as the only economic system that is consistent with the Bible."[166]

Making such a recommendation ignores the conflict between God's sovereignty and supremacy as taught in the Bible and the very project of socialist governments to set up "gods of their own." Writing against the French socialists of his day, Frederic Bastiat said, "Socialists want to play God," and they "look upon people as raw material to be formed into social combinations."[167]

Marx and Engels scoffed at those who warned that "Communism abolishes eternal truths; it abolishes all religion and morality." In the *Communist Manifesto,* they called this simply a "class antagonism," and a "bourgeois objection" to Communism.[168] Nevertheless, they, and all socialists like them, recognized that religion and morality *must* be abolished if they were to be successful in wooing the masses to their vision of re-creating a paradise on earth.[169] This vision is the "idolatry that overshadows all others," says David Horowitz. A former communist and radical activist himself, he tells it like it is. "When men put on the mantle of gods and attempt to remake the world in their own image, the results are hideous and destructive beyond conception."[170]

Socialism in every form is a "jealous god." It will not be opposed. It gives no place to any group that will not bend the knee under its control, whether that group be the Christian church in North Korea or the cult of the Falun Gong in Communist China.

The Harsh Reality of Socialism

The ministry of *The Voice of the Martyrs* continues to expose the persecution of Christians worldwide in totalitarian, communist, and Islamic states. Rev. Richard Wurmbrand founded the ministry as a voice for Christians who were being persecuted in communist nations, and the ministry brings Bibles and encouragement to Christians wherever they are being persecuted.

Wurmbrand himself spent 14 years in Romanian Communist prisons suffering beatings and torture. In 1948, the Communist regime of Romania launched a campaign against the Catholic and Greek-Catholic Uniate Churches of Romania. The regime imprisoned priests, closed churches and cathedrals, burned libraries, shut down schools, confiscated medical facilities and charities, and sent thousands of church members to prison.[171]

In Wurmbrand's view, Marx and his comrades were, strictly speaking, not atheists. Rather, "they openly denounced and reviled God; they hated a God in whom they believed. They challenged not his existence, but his supremacy." He noted that Marx praised the Communards of the French Revolution who boasted, "Our enemy is God. Hatred of God is the beginning of wisdom." Wurmbrand claimed that "a more equitable distribution of goods" or "better social institutions" were just "the outward trappings for concealing the real aim — the total eradication of God and His worship. We saw the evidence of this in such countries as Albania, and today in North Korea, where all churches, mosques, and pagodas have been closed."[172]

Joel McDurmon concurs with Wurmbrand's assessment. "It was the institution of this system that Marx saw, not as the product of, but as the means to abolishing religion itself."[173]

The communist nation of North Korea has topped the World Watch List produced by Open Doors USA for 14 consecutive years, and remains the "the worst place to be a Christian according to Open Doors, with 70,000 Christians estimated to be held in brutal labor camps."[174] The 2016 Open Doors report on North Korea states that "Christianity is not only seen as 'opium for the people,' as is normal for all communist states, it is also seen as deeply Western and despicable. Christians try to hide their faith as far as possible to avoid arrest and being sent to labor camps and horrific conditions."[175]

In 2010, Open Doors USA reported that in North Korea: "Christians are the target of fierce government action, and once caught, are not regarded as human. Last year we had evidence that some [of those captured] were used as guinea pigs to test chemical and biological weapons."[176] There is no indication this has changed.

The majority of the nations on the 2016 Watch List are Muslim states, but North Korea, China, and Vietnam are still listed. [177] China made headlines by modifying its draconian "One Child" policy. However, forced abortion and sterilization are still in

Richard Wurmbrand
(Voice of the Martyrs)

place. According to Human Rights Watch, when China's new leadership took power in 2013, they "unleashed an extraordinary assault on basic human rights."[178]

The total number of those killed by communist regimes during the twentieth century is estimated at over 100 million. The god of socialist states is not only jealous, it is cruel and merciless and seeks total control of those under its power.[179]

In 1938, Dorothy Thompson, an American journalist who was expelled from Germany, warned that National Socialism, like communism, should be seen as a secular religion that would not tolerate any rivals.[180]

It is likely that Christians were Hitler's ultimate target, says Bruce Walker in *The Swastika Against the Cross: The Nazi War on Christianity*. According to Walker, Hitler's war against the Jews was a "prelude" to the war he planned against Christians. During the 1930s, books were being written that forecast that Nazism would eradicate Christianity if it grew to dominate Europe.

Liberty, Virtue, and Religion

In contrast to the founders of the tyrannical regimes of communism and National Socialism, America's founders valued Christianity. They understood that the Christian religion promotes and encourages personal responsibility — a necessary condition for a free and self-governing people. Cultural analyst and Christian apologist Os Guinness explains this relationship:

> [T]he American framers' linking of republicanism and religion was one of their most characteristic, if surprising, emphases. They believed that the self-government of the republic rests on the self-government of the citizens. They recognized that the rule of law constrains the external, whereas an individual's faith is obedience to the unenforceable and an act of freedom. Faith is indispensable to freedom, they claimed — to liberty itself, and also to the

Os Guinness

> social vitality and civic harmony that under-
> gird freedom. Their position can be expressed
> simply in a kind of eternal triangle of first prin-
> ciples: "liberty requires virtue, virtue requires
> religion, and religion requires liberty."[181]

This relationship between liberty, virtue, and religion is completely foreign to the thinking of socialists, who despise religion, deny the need for virtue, and have no use for liberty other than the freedom they seek to pursue their own ends of domination and control.

Some within the church argue that capitalism "has demonstrated its inability to satisfy the basic needs of humans."[182] Therefore, they argue, the church must turn to Marxist theory for solutions to economic disparities. However, in spite of such efforts to reconcile Marxist socialism with Christian beliefs, one inescapable fact remains: Wherever Marxism and socialism have gained control, the Christian church has come under attack and suffered persecution.

The harsh reality is that socialism is at war with the true Church of Jesus Christ. When socialists gain control, virtue, liberty, and religion rarely survive.

—Karen VanTil Gushta

TRUTH 10

Socialism Creates Refugees

"It is the government who is responsible for my wife's death, not the doctors."

—*Jose Perez, 63 year-old Venezuelan whose wife died because of a shortage of medical supplies.*[183]

During the 20th century, except for brief periods of democratic government, the Venezuelan economy suffered under the rule of various strongmen presidents. However, when Venezuelans elected Hugo Chavez as president in 1998, following collapse of confidence in the existing political parties, the economy became even more depressed. Chavez established his United Socialist Party, seized control of key economic sectors, and announced increased spending on social programs by means of redistribution of the country's oil wealth. His intention, he declared, was to take Venezuela down a path similar to Cuba's. [184]

Venezuela now has the weakest property rights in the world and inflation is running at nearly 100 percent. [185]

Refugees often become one of the chief exports of nations that come under socialist control. As governments centralize economic planning and take over industries, food shortages and rationing become commonplace. Restrictions on basic freedoms send people fleeing to find a better life elsewhere. Venezuela is a prime example of this. The number of foreign-born Venezuelans in the U.S. grew by 388 percent from 35,000 in 1990

to 170,000 in 2013 according to the Pew Research Center's "Hispanic Trends."[186] So many have settled in the South Florida community of Weston that some now know it as "Westonzuela."

Fleeing Castro

Another example is the regime of Cuban dictator Fidel Castro, idolized by Chávez. In 1960, the year after the Cuban Revolution propelled Castro to power, the dictator began to nationalize foreign and Cuban-owned businesses on the Caribbean island.[187] He seized power in other ways as well:

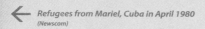

> The freedom of the press, freedom of assembly, the right to a writ of habeas corpus, and the University of Havana's autonomy were destroyed. The Castro regime intervened in and either shut down or revolutionized the labor unions, professional associations, private clubs, and, in 1961, Cuba's public and private school system.[188]

Finally, on April 16, 1961, Castro declared Cuba a Socialist State. Parents who feared their children would be taught Marxist ideology rushed them onto planes bound for the U.S. under a Catholic Church-led refugee program dubbed Operation Pedro Pan. Some 14,000 children were evacuated and sent to Miami between 1960 and 1962.[189]

Thousands of Cubans headed for Florida, a mere 90 miles away, to escape "the establishment of a totalitarian Communist state personified by Fidel Castro." By the end of the 1960s, a whopping 500,000 Cubans had left the Caribbean nation.[190] Many more would flee, including 125,000 who packed into boats in 1980 during the Mariel boatlift episode. Altogether, more than 800,000 Cubans sought asylum in the U.S. by 1990.[191] Today, back in Cuba, the drop in the birth rate is among the largest in the Western Hemisphere, as despairing Cubans make use of unrestricted access to legal abortion.[192]

Fleeing the Sandinistas

At the height of Fidel Castro's reign, rebel movements in Central America "were influenced, and to some extent supported, by the communist regime in Cuba."[193] Consequently, in 1979 when Nicaragua's Sandinista fighters deposed the right-wing government led by Anastasio Somoza, the country inherited a socialist government.

> Instead of a new-found stability, [Nicaragua] descended deeper into the morass of civil war as the hard-line Marxist faction of the Sandinista Front won the upper hand for control.[194]

About 100,000 wealthy Nicaraguans fled.[195] By the end of the 1980s, 50,000 more Nicaraguans had left for Honduras and roughly 40,000 for Costa Rica, many of them Miskito Indians.[196]

Fidel Castro
(Scott McKieman/Zuma)

Jews and East Germans

Germans fled socialist regimes in the Fatherland twice in the twentieth century. The first wave began in the 1930s. At that time, Nazi policies were not so much about nationalizing private businesses as they were about promoting nationalism and establishing a single national identity — Jews excluded. In 1935, the Nazis (the National Socialist German Workers' Party) adopted the Nuremberg laws, striking the citizenship rights of Jews. The Third Reich then pushed Jews even further to the edge, encouraging German employers to dismiss Jewish employees and urging boycotts of Jewish businesses.[197]

Those Jews who could, fled the country. From 1933 to 1935, aid agencies helped resettle 80,000 Jewish refugees in Palestine and elsewhere.[198] Some headed to France, and others to "places no one ever heard of before — Ecuador, Bolivia, Shanghai, the Dominican Republic. There were endless lines in front of the foreign embassies and consulates in Berlin."[199] So immense was the dispersion that "there was not a country in which not at least a few refugees could be found."[200]

Between the Nazi's rise to power in 1933 and Nazi Germany's surrender in 1945, more than 340,000 Jews emigrated from Germany and Austria. In one two-year time span, 85,000 resettled in the U.S.[201] Millions of others, who had been rounded up and hauled off to Nazi extermination camps, were never seen again. At war's end, the Allied forces split Germany into two blocs, with the U.S. and Britain controlling the West, and the Soviet Union the East. Walter Ulbricht, the head of the ruling Socialist Unity

*Germans flee communist East Germany on July 31, 1961,
just before East Berlin's partition.*
(DPA/Zuma)

Party (SED) in East Germany, called for a "systematic implementation of Socialism,"[202] which created a second wave of German refugees.

In true "bureaucratic, collectivist" style, East Germany's SED exercised unbridled state intervention.[203] The ruling body turned all levels of education, from day care to adult, into instruments of ideological instruction.[204] Organizations and trade unions flourished, but were mere outlets for socialist indoctrination. Meanwhile, private industry was swallowed up, "so that the bulk of production was owned either by 'the people' (that is, the state) or in some form of joint ownership with state participation."[205] Consequently, by the time East Germany built the Berlin Wall in 1961, two million refugees had already abandoned the East's socialism for the capitalist West.[206]

Fleeing the Vietcong

> "What was the one event during the trip [evacuation] you will never forget," an interviewer asked a Vietnamese woman en route...to the U.S. "It was when all of these people were trying to get on the plane at the airport," she replied. "I saw the people jamming the door and women and children could not get on. The shelling came closer and then the plane took off with people hanging at the door."[207]

NORTH KOREA

Over 2.5 million people died during widespread famine in the 1990s. Today, close to 60 percent of the population does not have enough food to stay healthy. Seventy percent of children under age six are malnourished.

Before North Vietnam's communist forces marched into Saigon on April 30, 1975, refugees numbering 140,000 — most with close ties to the former South Vietnam government — were evacuated and resettled in the U.S.[208] The horrific account above represents only one of the thousands of harrowing refugee stories. Upon the arrival of the Communist North Vietnamese Army and Vietcong, South Vietnamese took to boats — however leaky — and headed for neighboring Thailand (5,000 refugees), Hong Kong (4,000), Singapore (1,800), and the Philippines (1,250).[209] They risked death at sea, unpredictable storms, and attacks from pirates, who raided fleeing vessels and raped their women.

In the shadows of this human tragedy, the communist leadership in Hanoi unified North and South Vietnam as the

Socialist Republic of Vietnam in July 1976. The leadership's socialist goals, however, clashed with the ethnic Chinese population's dominance in the private economic sector.[210] More than 250,000 Vietnamese of Chinese origin fled to China, forced out by harsh economic policies and the government's confiscation of their businesses.[211] The flow of refugees leaving South Vietnam continued into 1978 — when countries in Southeast Asia hosted 62,000 Vietnamese "boat people" in camps. In the two decades that followed, the U.S. opened its doors to 500,000 Vietnamese people.[212]

North Korea — A Nation Like a Prison

If ever a country were a prison, North Korea would be it. Overseeing its almost 25 million "inmates" is the hereditary "supreme leader" Kim Jong-un. His grandfather, Kim Il-sung, was supreme leader for 46 years and turned North Korea into a socialist state, supported economically by the Soviet Union. When the USSR collapsed, so did North Korea's economy and poverty and famine have plagued the nation ever since. [213]

Over 2.5 million people died during widespread famine in the 1990s. Today, close to 60 percent of the population does not have enough food to stay healthy. Seventy percent of children under age six are malnourished.[214]

In 2014, Kim Jong-un ordered 33 Christians, believed to be working alongside a South Korean Baptist missionary, to be put to death. **Nevertheless, the blood of the martyrs continues to be the seed of the church.**

Those who manage to escape the totalitarian rule and make it past the heavily patrolled border "take a long and risky land journey through China to Thailand, Vietnam, Cambodia and other Southeast Asian countries on their way to eventual asylum in South Korea."[215]

Overwhelmed by their numbers, the Chinese government erected a massive barbed wire and concrete fence along a stretch of the Yalu River bordering the countries to keep refugees out. Three years ago, North Korea reportedly began erecting a fence to keep them in. Some 27,000 North Koreans have defected to the South.[216]

But not all who leave the impoverished communist nation desire the same thing. While many North Koreans head to China to save their lives, Christians often risk the trip to study the Bible. They receive instruction in underground Bible schools and are sometimes willing to smuggle a Bible or other Christian literature back into North Korea, activities for which they could be executed.[217]

Kim Jong-un has followed his family tradition of persecuting Christians. In 2014, he ordered 33 Christians believed to be working alongside a South Korean Baptists missionary to be put to death. Nevertheless, the blood of the martyrs continues to be the seed of the church, and this missionary reportedly planted 500 underground churches before his arrest in 2013.[218]

Socialism often creates refugees, and at its worst, it produces a grisly body count.

As socialism creeps across America's horizon, the words of Kitty Werthmann, age 12 when Hitler took over Austria, say it best: "After America, there is no place to run."[219]

—Andrew Scott

CONCLUSION

We Have to Reverse Course

We didn't know it at the time but when Alexander Solzhenitsyn gave his famous commencement address "A World Split Apart," at Harvard University in June 1978, the Soviet Union was in its long, dying phase. Not only were its leaders — Brezhnev, Chernenko, Andropov — dying, so was the empire they led.

Solzhenitsyn, who chronicled the long terror that enveloped Russia in his magnum opus *The Gulag Archipelago*, written in the late '50s and early '60s and published in the West in 1973, offered this explanation for the moral confusion that even the West was beginning to suffer:

> Such a tilt of freedom in the direction of evil has come about gradually but it was evidently born primarily out of a humanistic and benevolent concept according to which there is no evil inherent to human nature; the world belongs to mankind and all the defects of life are caused by wrong social systems which must be corrected.[220]

Alexander Solzhenitsyn
(Newscom)

In another venue, he put it even more succinctly:

> **Men have forgotten God; that's why all this has happened.**[221]

Jesus said, out of the heart a man speaks, and socialism is an elaborate socio-economic structure that arises largely out of a heart of envy. It's not fair that you have more than I do. I want it (or at least some of it) and you must either give it or I'll take it from you — at the point of a gun. If it is the government pointing the gun, then I'm not morally culpable for taking it from you.

But socialism's lure goes even deeper than envy. By replacing God's rules with man's own, it frees man to pursue any vice he desires. So socialism is at bottom, a rebellion against God and God's clear words regarding morality and economics. That's why so many of the socialist philosophers were virulently atheist or tried to co-opt God in their versions of man-made paradise.

The problem is that when man becomes a law unto himself, he winds up under other men's tyranny. Unrestrained by the biblical, leveling notion of an Almighty God who will judge everyone's actions upon death, the makers of heaven on Earth will do anything to bring about their vision, up to and including theft, torture and mass murder. As we have seen in this book, history is replete with evidence of this.

So why are we, as Americans, going down this road? That is the ultimate question posed by this book. Will America align itself with the failed socialist policies of the past — or will we correct course and return to the God Who made Heaven and Earth?

"We have to reverse course," said former Minnesota Representative Michele Bachmann, who was one of the most forceful advocates of free enterprise in Congress. **"What we have to do is get government out of private industry. . . . We need to reverse course, so that we can get back to freedom."**[222]

America has a great opportunity to learn from Europe and other countries that have succumbed to socialism's siren song of abandoning personal responsibility for cradle-to-grave welfare. But it's not enough to know the facts and history of socialism's tyrannical rule. The problem lies in the unregenerate human heart, which, without God's illumination, is easily fooled and manipulated.

All of us who value freedom face an enormous challenge if America is going to remain a self-governing, free nation. Our constitutional republic is in jeopardy. Government has become god in the minds of many, and they look to it, not the true God, as the provider for all their needs and many of their wants. A generation of young people has been indoctrinated to accept

Dr. D. James Kennedy

socialism as a desirable form of government. And a self-pro-claimed "democratic socialist" is making headway as a possible presidential nominee.

Dr. D. James Kennedy outlined the challenge we face:

> Only Christ can open the eyes of people and make them see what the signs of the times are. Only Christ can give people the moral courage to take the kinds of stands necessary to take in the very critical period in which we live. Have you found that courage? Do you have that faith that will enable you to be willing to say with Patrick Henry, "Give me liberty, or give me death"? Unless enough Americans have that faith and that courage, this nation will surely fall.

But, Dr. Kennedy added, "if we have that faith and courage, America will grow stronger, and the cor-rupt and rotten system of communism will continue to grow weaker.... [I]t will dry up and wither until it finally disappears."[223]

These words were spoken in 1987, just two years before the Soviet empire collapsed. What was true then is just as true today—if not more so.

We must turn to Christ for the moral courage to stand for liberty and the true principles upon which our nation was founded. And we must pray that Christ will open the eyes of the people "and make them see what the signs of the times are." Too many are succumbing to the enticing call for a "strong leader" to "make America great again." Whatever greatness America has had in the past only came because it was founded upon and following the moral principles of Christianity. There can be no hope of restoring America's greatness if our nation does not return to those principles and repent of our national sins.

However, if we, as followers of Christ, rise to the present challenge, and act, not out of fear, but with faith and courage and humble reliance on God, repenting of our own sins, God may in His mercy restore America to her former position as "a city upon a hill," where righteousness rules and freedom is treasured.

ENDNOTES

1   Joshua Muravchik, *Heaven on Earth: The Rise and Fall of Socialism* (San Francisco: Encounter Books, 2002), p. 3.

2   "A New Era of Responsibility: Renewing America's Promise," Office of Management and Budget, p. 9. At http://www.gpoaccess.gov/usbudget/fy10/pdf/fy10-newera.pdf.

3   Daniel Henninger, "Obama's Business Buyout," *Wall Street Journal*, Feb. 24, 2010. At http://online.wsj.com/article/SB10001424052748704240004575085691881400382.html.

4   Coral Ridge Ministries interview with Rep. Michele Bachmann on Feb. 5, 2010.

5   See F. A. Hayek, *The Road to Serfdom*, ed. by Bruce Caldwell (University of Chicago Press, 2007).

6   Albert Fried and Ronald Sanders, *Socialist Thought: A Documentary History* (Garden City, New York: Anchor Books, Doubleday, 1964), p. 3.

7   Jean-Jacques Rousseau, *The Social Contract and Discourse on the Origin of Inequality*, edited by Lester G. Crocker (New York: Washington Square Press, Simon & Schuster, 1967).

8   Richard Grenier, *Capturing the Culture: Film, Art, and Politics* (Washington, D.C.: Ethics and Public Policy Center, 1991), p. 324.

9   Vladimir Lenin, *"Left-Wing" Communism, an Infantile Disorder*, April-May 1920, (Peking, China: FLP, 1970), quoted in J.V. Stalin, *The Foundations of Leninism* (Peking, China: Foreign Languages Press reprint, 1975), p. 44, originally in Joseph Stalin, *Works* (Moscow: Foreign Languages Publishing House, Vol. 6, 1953).

10 See Mark Kramer, et al, *The Black Book of Communism: Crimes, Terror, Repression* (Cambridge, Mass.: The President and Fellows of Harvard College, 1999), and Robert Conquest, *The Great Terror: A Reassessment* (Oxford University Press, 40th Anniversary edition, 2007).

11 See William L. Shirer, *The Rise and Fall of the Third Reich*: A History of Nazi Germany (New York: Simon And Schuster, 1960).

12 Ibid.

13 Muravchik, *Heaven on Earth*, pp. 105-06.

14 Karl Marx and Friedrich Engels, *The Communist Manifesto*, p 49.

15 Ibid., p. 48.

16 Friedrich Engels, *Origins of the Family, Private Property and the State*, "The Monogamous Family" in Chapter Two, The Family, Marx/Engels Selected Works, Vol. 3, Marx/Engels Internet Archive, at http://www.marxists.org/archive/marx/works/1884/origin-family/ch02d.htm.

17 See Robert Knight, *Fighting for America's Soul: How Sweeping Change Threatens Our Nation and What We Must Do* (Fort Lauderdale: Coral Ridge Ministries, 2009), pp. 43-50.

18 John Quincy Adams, as quoted in Jerry Newcombe, *The Book That Made America* (Ventura, Calif.: Nordskog Publishing, 2009), p. 158.

19 Jeffrey Collins, "The Art of Being Ruled," a book review of *Hobbes and the Law of Nature* by Perez Zagorin, *The Wall Street Journal*, Feb. 18, 2010, A-17.

20 Quoted in Robert Knight, *The Age of Consent: The Rise of Relativism and the Corruption of Popular Culture* (Dallas: Spence Publishing Company, 1998, 2000), p. 33.

21 Quoted in *Socialist Thought*, 78.

22 James H. Billington, *Fire in the Minds of Men: Origins of the Revolutionary Faith* (New York: Basic Books, 1980), p. 25.

23 Ibid., pp. 31, 32.

24 Ibid., p. 255.

25 Ibid., p. 252.

26 Ibid.

27 Muravchik, *Heaven on Earth*, pp. 31-59.

28 Steven Kreis, "Robert Owen, 1771-1858" in *The History Guide: Lectures on Modern European Intellectual History*, at http://www.historyguide.org/intellect/owen.html.

29 Friedrich Engels, To Friedrich Graeber in Berlin, July 12, 1839, *Letters of Friedrich Engels*, at Marx/Engels Archive, at http://www.marxists.org/archive/marx/works/1839/letters/39_07_12.htm.

30 Frederich Engels, *Origins of the Family, Private Property and the State*, "The Monogamous Family" in Chapter Two, The Family, *Marx/Engels Selected Works*, Vol. 3, Marx/Engels Internet Archive, at http://www.marxists.org/archive/marx/works/1884/origin-family/ch02d.htm.

31 Harry J. Carroll, et al, *The Development of Civilization: A Documentary History of Politics, Society and Thought* (Chicago: Scott, Foresman and Company, 1962), p. 215.

32 Ibid., pp. 214-215.

33 See, for instance, Jean-Michel Angebert, *The Occult and the Third Reich* (New York: Macmillan Publishing Co., Inc., 1974).

34 William L. Shirer, *The Rise and Fall of the Third Reich: A History of Nazi Germany* (New York: Simon and Schuster, 1960), p. 100.

35 Ibid.

36 Robert G.L. Waite, *The Psychopathic God—Adolf Hitler* (New York: Basic Books, 1977), quoted in Joseph J. Carr, *The Twisted Cross: The Occultic Religion of Hitler and the New Age Nazism of the Third Reich* (Lafayette, La.: Huntington House Publishers, 1985), p. 39.

37 Mao Tse-Tung, *The Foolish Old Man Who Removed the Mountains, Selected Works*, Vol. III, June 11, 1945, p. 322, quoted in *Quotations from Chairman Mao Tse-Tung* (United States Edition, New York: Bantam Books, 1967), p. 114.

38 Mao Tse-Tung, *Serve the People, Selected Works*, Sept. 8, 1944, Vol. III, 227, cited in *Quotations*, p. 97.

39 Thomas Jefferson, letter to Joseph Milligan, April 6, 1818, quoted in Conservative Colloquium at www.conservativecolloquium.wordpress.com/2007/11/24/founding-fathers-on-charity-wealth-redistribution-and-federal-govt and referenced in Bill Wilson's blog, *The Daily Jot*, March 10, 2010.

40 P.J. O'Rourke Quotes at http://homepage.eircom.net/%257Eodyssey/Politics/Liberty/PJ.html,

41 Jennifer Bendery, "Bernie Sanders: What's Wrong With America Looking More Like Scandinavia?" *HuffingtonPost.com*, May 4, 2015, http://www.huffingtonpost.com/2015/05/03/bernie-sanders-campaign_n_7199546.html (accessed February 18, 2016).

42 "Bernie Sanders is Not a Social Democrat; He's a Marxist," John C. Goodman, *Townhall.com*, February 13, 2016, http://townhall.com/columnists/johncgoodman/2016/02/13/bernie-sanders-is-not-a-social-democrat-hes-a-marxist-n2118509 (accessed February 16, 2016).

43 Joseph Sobran, "*Pensees*: Notes for the reactionary of tomorrow," *National Review*, Dec. 31, 1985, p. 36.

44 Robert Heilbroner, quoted in *Pensees*, p. 36.

45 Vladimir Ilyich Lenin, quoted in J.V. Stalin, *The Foundations of Leninism*, originally published in Moscow as part of Stalin's *Works*, Foreign Languages Publishing House, Vol. 6, 1953, and later by Foreign Languages Press, Peking, China, 1975, p. 45.

46 Robert Conquest, *The Harvest of Sorrow: Soviet Collectivization and the Terror-Famine* (University of Alberta Press, 1986), excerpt at http://www.ditext.com/conquest/16.html.

47 Mao Tse-Tung, "Problems of War and Strategy," *Selected Works*, Vol. II, p. 224, Nov. 6, 1938, in *Quotations from Chairman Mao Tse-Tung*, p. 33.

48 Stephane Courtois, Nicolas Werth, Jean-Louis Panne, Andrzej Paczkowski, Karel Bartosek, Jean-Louis Margolin, translated by Jonathan Murphy and Mark Kramer, *The Black Book of Communism: Crimes, Terror, Repression* (President and Fellows of Harvard College, 1999), p. 4, at http://www.amazon.com/

Black-Book-Communism-Crimes Repression/dp/0674076087#reader_0674076087.

49 Steve Waldman, "Obama Wields the Bible Against Socialist Charge," BeliefNet, October 31, 2008, at http://blog.beliefnet.com/stevenwaldman/2008/10/obama-wields-the-bible-against.html.

50 Karl Marx and Frederick Engels, *Collected Works*, forty volumes (New York: International Publishers, 1976), vol. 3, p. 399. Quoted in David A. Noebel, *Understanding the Times: The Religious Worldviews of Our Day and the Search for Truth* (Eugene, Ore.: Harvest House Publishers, Inc., 1991), p. 715.

51 David Aikman, *The Delusion of Disbelief* (Carol Stream, Ill: SaltRiver, 2008), 106–107. Quoted in Joel McDurmon, "Spurgeon On Socialism," American Vision, March 6, 2009, at http://www.americanvision.org/article/spurgeon-on-socialism/.

52 Karl Marx and Frederick Engels, *Manifesto of the Communist Party* (Marxists Internet Archive, marxists.org,, 2000) p. 20, at http://www.marxists.org/archive/marx/works/download/manifest.pdf.

53 Laidler, *History of Socialism*, p. 384. Quoted in Noebel, *Understanding the Times: The Religious Worldviews of Our Day and the Search for Truth*, p. 686.

54 Merriam-Webster's Collegiate Dictionary. Eleventh ed. (Springfield, Mass.: Merriam-Webster, Inc., 2003). Entry for "Socialism."

55 Frederic Bastiat, *The Law*, translated by Dean Russell, (Irvington-on-Hudson, NY: The Foundation for Economic Education, Inc., 1998), p. 18.

56 Joel McDurmon, God Versus Socialism, (Powder Springs, Ga: American Vision, 2009), p. 6-7.

57 Calvin Beisner, *Prosperity and Poverty: The Compassionate Use of Resources in a World of Scarcity* (Westchester, Ill: Crossway, 1986), p. 73. Quoted in David A. Noebel, *Understanding the Times: The Religious Worldviews of Our Day and the Search for Truth* (Eugene, Ore: Harvest House Publishers, Inc., 1991), p. 698.

58 Marx and Engels, *Manifesto of the Communist Party*, p. 32.

59 Ibid., p. 13.

60 Strachey, *The Theory and Practice of Socialism* (New York: Random House, 1936), title page. Quoted in David A. Noebel, *Understanding the Times: The Religious Worldviews of Our Day and the Search for Truth* (Eugene, Ore: Harvest House Publishers, Inc., 1991), p. 689.

61 Mark Kramer, Stephane Courtois, Jean-Louis Panne, Andrzej Paczkowski, Karel Bartosek, Jean-Louis Margolin, *The Black Book of Communism: Crimes, Terror, Repression* (Harvard University Press, 1999), p. x.

62 Lenin, *Collected Works*, vol. 26, pp. 414-15. Quoted in Noebel, *Understanding the Times*, p. 687.

63 Moses Hess, *A Communist Confession of Faith*, 1846. Quoted in Joshua Muravchik, *Heaven on Earth: The Rise and Fall of Socialism* (San Francisco: Encounter Books, 2002).

64 D. James Kennedy, *The Mortgaging of America* (Fort Lauderdale, Fla.: Coral Ridge Ministries, 2009), p. 19.

65 Jeffrey M. Jones and Daniel Heil, "The Politics of Envy," *Hoover Digest*, 2009, No. 2, at http://www.hoover.org/publications/digest/42922687.html.

66 Kant, *Metaphysics of Morals*. Quoted in Jones and Heil, "The Politics of Envy."

67 Ibid.

68 Quoted in Joseph Epstein, *Envy: The Seven Deadly Sins*, (Oxford: Oxford University Press, 2003), p. 6.

69 Alexis de Tocqueville, *Democracy in America*, translated by Harvey C. Mansfield and Delba Winthrop, (Chicago, Ill.: University of Chicago Press, 2000), p. 189.

70 Ibid., p. 9.

71 Ibid., p. 14.

72 Tommy Newberry, *The War on Success: How the Obama Agenda Is Shattering the American Dream*, (Washington, D.C., Regnery Publishing, Inc., 2010), p. 54.

73 Ibid.

74   Ibid.

75   Jones and Heil, "The Politics of Envy."

76   Ronald H. Nash, *Poverty and Wealth: Why Socialism Doesn't Work,* (Richardson, Tex.: Word Publishing, 1986), pp. 57-58.

77   Jay W. Richards, *Money, Greed, and God: Why Capitalism Is the Solution and Not the Problem,* (New York: Harper Collins Publishers, 2009), p. 4.

78   Paul Greenberg, "Politics of Envy," Tribune Media Services, Inc., November 8, 2007, at http://www.nysun. com/opinion/politics-of-envy/66096.

79   Jeffrey M. Jones and Daniel Heil, "The Politics of Envy," *Hoover Digest,* 2009, No. 2, at http://www.hoover. org/publications/digest/42922687.html.

80   Ibid.

81   Linda Chavez, "Politics of Envy," *Human Events.com,* October 23, 2009, at http://www.humanevents. com/article.php?id=34101.

82   Walter Williams, "Who Poses the Greater Threat?" *Townhall.com,* March 3, 2010, at http://townhall.com/ columnists/WalterEWilliams/2010/03/03/who_poses_the_greater_threat.

83   Quotes from 2001 interview on Chicago's WBEZ-FM, October 30, 2008. Quoted in Jim DeMint, *Saving Freedom: We Can Stop America's Slide into Socialism,* (Nashville, Tenn.: B&H Publishing Group, 2009), p. 191.

84   Ibid.

85   Frederic Bastiat, *The Law,* translated by Dean Russell, (Irvington-on-Hudson, NY: The Foundation for Economic Education, 1998), p. 13.

86   David Schweickart, "On Socialist Envy," paper presented at the Sixth Conference of No. American and Cuban Philosophers, Havana, Cuba, June 16, 1994. at http://www.luc.edu/faculty/dschwei/socenvy.pdf.

87   D. James Kennedy, *The Mortgaging of America: Biblical Wisdom for a Time of Uncertainty and Change,* (Ft. Lauderdale, Fla.: Coral Ridge Ministries Media, Inc., 2009), p. 47.

88   Ibid., p. 48.

89   Quoted in Edward Eggleston, *A History of Life in the United States* (New York: D. Appleton & Company, 1897), p. 28.

90   From "The Description of Virginia by Captain Smith," in *Narratives of Early Virginia, 1606-1625*, ed. by Lyon Gardiner Tayler, LL.D., p. 81.

91   Edward Eggleston, *A History of Life in the United States* (New York: D. Appleton & Company, 1897), p. 39.

92   Eggleston, *A History of Life*, p. 40.

93   Benjamin Hart, *Faith and Freedom: The Christian Roots of American Liberty* (San Bernardino, Calif.: Here's Life Publishers, Inc., 1988), p. 143.

94   Eggleston, *A History of Life*, p. 26.

95   *The Jamestown adventure: accounts of the Virginia colony, 1605-1614*, ed. by Ed Southern. (Winston-Salem, North Carolina: John F. Blair, Publishers, 2004), p. 199.

96   Eggleston, *A History of Life*, p. 179.

97   William Bradford, *Of Plymouth Plantation*, ed. Samuel Eliot Morison (New York: Alfred A. Knopf, 1952), p. 121.

98   William Bradford, *Of Plymouth Plantation* (New York: The Modern Library, 1952), p. 120. Quoted in D. James Kennedy, Ph.D., with Charles Hull Wolfe, Ph.D., *Restoring the Real Meaning of Thanksgiving* (Fort Lauderdale, Fla.: Coral Ridge Ministries, 1989, 2003), p. 19.

99   D. James Kennedy, Ph.D., with Charles Hull Wolfe, Ph.D., *Restoring the Real Meaning of Thanksgiving* (Fort Lauderdale, Fla.: Coral Ridge Ministries, 1989, 2003), p. 19.

100 William Bradford, *Of Plymouth Plantation*, ed. Samuel Eliot Morison (New York: Alfred A. Knopf, 1952), p. 132.

101 James Truslow Adams, *The Founding of New England* (Boston: Atlantic Monthly Press, 1921), p. 116.

102 William Bradford, *Of Plymouth Plantation*, ed. Samuel Eliot Morison (New York: Alfred A. Knopf, 1952), p. 120-21.

103 Ibid., p. 121 (emphasis added).

104 Peter J. Boettke and Peter T. Leeson, *Socialism: Still Impossible After All These Years*, p. 12, at Monograph at http://mises.org/journals/scholar/Boettke.pdf.

105 *The Russian Revolution 1917-1921*, (1935, vol. 2, 105). Quoted in Boettke and Leeson, *Socialism*, pp. 16-17.

106 Robert Heilbroner, Socialism, The Concise Encyclopedia of Economics, at http://www.econlib.org/library/Enc/Socialism.html.

107 Joshua Muravchik, *Heaven on Earth: The Rise and Fall of Socialism* (San Francisco: Encounter Books, 2002), p. 275.

108 Ibid., pp. 198-226.

109 Interview, Rev. Christopher Mtikila, National Chairman, Democratic Party of Tanzania, Pastor, Full Salvation Church, at http://www.pbs.org/heavenonearth/interviews_mtikila.html.

110 Muravchik, *Heaven on Earth*, p. 221.

111 Muravchik, *Heaven on Earth*, p. 224.

112 P. J. O'Rourke, *Eat the Rich: A Treatise on Economics* (Atlantic Monthly Press, 1999), p. 177.

113 Muravchik, *Heaven on Earth*., p. 225.

114 Swaminathan S. Anklesaria Aiyar, "Market Capitalism Beats Bolivarian Socialism," Cato Institute, at http://www.cato.org/pub_display.php?pub_id=10062.

115 Daniel Wagner and C. J. Redfern, "21st Century Socialism's Impact on Latin American Economic Performance," Huffington Post, December 1, 2009, at http://www.huffingtonpost.com/daniel-wagner/21st-century-socialisms-i_b_375277.html.

116 Richard W. Rahn, "The Swedish Model," Cato Institute, at http://www.cato.org/pub_display.php?pub_id=10462.

117 Martin De Vlieghere, "The Myth of the Scandinavian Model," *The Brussels Journal*, November 25, 2005, at http://www.brusselsjournal.com/node/510.

118 "2016 Index of Economic Freedom," *The Heritage Foundation*, http://www.heritage.org/index/ranking (accessed February 18, 2016).

119 Mark J. Perry, "Why Socialism Failed," *The Freeman*, June 1995, Vol. 45, Issue 6, at http://www.thefreemanonline.org/featured/why-socialism-failed/.

120 *Ludwig von Mises, Economic Calculation in the Socialist Commonwealth*, p. 17, at http://mises.org/pdf/econcalc.pdf.

121 See Hans-Hermann Hoppe, *A Theory of Socialism and Capitalism: Economics, Politics, and Ethics* (Boston/Dordrecht/London: Kluwer Academic Publishers, 1989).

122 Tom G. Palmer, "Why Socialism Collapsed in Eastern Europe," *Cato Policy Report*, September/October 1990, at http://www.cato.org/pub_display.php?pub_id=6007.

123 Wagner and Redfern, "21st Century Socialism's Impact" at http://www.huffingtonpost.com/daniel-wagner/21st-century-socialisms-i_b_375277.html.

124 Milton Friedman, "We Have Socialism, Q.E.D." *The New York Times*, December 31, 1989, at http://www.nytimes.com/2008/10/19/opinion/19opclassic.html.

125 Perry, "Why Socialism Failed," at http://www.thefreemanonline.org/featured/why-socialism-failed/.

126 Homeschooling Family Granted Political Asylum," Homeschool Legal Defense Association, January 26, 2010, at:http://www.hslda.org/hs/international/Germany/201001260.asp.

127 Quoted in Duane Lester, "The Threats to Homeschooling: From Hitler to the NEA," August 11, 2008, at http://www.allamericanblogger.com/3415/the-threats-to-homeschooling-from-hitler-to-the-nea/.

128 Interview with John Rabe, Coral Ridge Ministries Media, Inc. June 1, 2009.

129 Robert H. Knight, *Fighting for America's Soul,* (Fort Lauderdale, Fla: Coral Ridge Ministries Media, Inc., 2009), p. 43.

130 Erwin W. Lutzer, *When a Nation Forgets God: 7 Lessons We Must Learn From Nazi Germany.* (Chicago, Ill.: Moody Press, 2010), pp. 101-102.

131 William S. Lind, "Who Stole Our Culture?" quoted in David Kupelian, "The Blur," *Whistleblower,* May 2015, p. 17.

132 David Kupelian, "'Thought Police' in the Age of Obama," *Whistleblower,* September 2015, p. 10.

133 Katie McDonough, "Bernie Sanders killed it with young voters in New Hampshire—including a huge majority of young women," *Fusion.net,* February 9, 2016, http://fusion.net/story/266702/bernie-sand ers-new-hampshire-primary-win-young-voters/ (accessed February 17, 2016).

134 "Sexual liberation and the Russian Revolution," Socialist Worker Online, archive, dated 20 January 2007, issue 2034, at http://www.socialistworker.co.uk/art.php?id=10491.

135 Kitty Werthmann, "Lesson from Austria, Would You Vote for Hitler? The testimony of Kitty Werthmann," at http://groups.google.com/group/misc.legal/msg/723471b488748596, accessed 2/26/2010.

136 Ibid.

137 Robert H. Bork, *Slouching Towards Gomorrah,* (New York: Harper Collins, 1996), p. 159.

138 Linda Chavez, "Abstinence Education Works After All," *Human Events.com,* 2/5/2010, at http://www.humanevents.com/article.php?id=35513.

139 Miriam Grossman, *You're Teaching My Child What? A Physician Exposes the Lies of Sex Education and How They Harm Your Child,* (Washington D.C.: Regnery, 2009), p. 15.

140 Ibid., pp. 28-30.

141 Frank York and Jan LaRue, *Protecting Your Child in an X-Rated World: What You Need to Know to Make a Difference,* (Wheaton, Ill.: Tyndale House Publishers, Inc., 2002), p. 63.

142 Timothy Matthews, "The Frankfurt School: Conspiracy to Corrupt," *Catholic Insight,* March, 2009, at http://catholicinsight.com/online/features/article_882.shtml.

143 Steven Erlanger, "UN Guide for Sex Ed Generates Opposition," *New York Times,* September 2, 2009, at: http://www.nytimes.com/2009/09/03/world/03unesco.html?_r=1

144 Kathleen Farah, "Girl Scouts Taught How to be 'Hot'," WorldNetDaily.com, March 16, 2010, at: http:// www.wnd.com/index.php?fa=PAGE.view&pageId=128389 Drew Zahn, "Girl Scouts Hiding Secret Sex Agenda?" WorldNetDaily.com, March 19, 2010, at: http://www.wnd.com/index.php?fa=PAGE. view&pageId=129757

145 "Healthy, Happy, and Hot," International Planned Parenthood Federation brochure, p. 7, at http:// www.ippf.org/NR/rdonlyres/B4462DDE-487D-4194-B0E0-193A04095819/0/HappyHealthyHot.pdf.

146 Lutzer, *When a Nation Forgets God,* p. 114.

147 *Stone v. Graham,* 449 U.S. p. 39 (1980).

148 Irving Kristol, "Countercultures: Past, Present, and Future." January 10, 1994, AEI Bradley Lecture Series, at http://www.aei.org/speech/17980.

149 Karl Marx and Friedrich Engels, *The Communist Manifesto,* (Filiquarian Publishing, LLC, 2005), pp. 39-30. at http://www.amazon.com/Communist-Manifesto-Complete-Published-Prefaces/dp/1599869950/ref =sr_1_1?ie=UTF8&s=books&qid=1268765150&sr=1-1#reader_1599869950.

150 Allan C. Carlson, "The Family in America: Retrospective and Prospective," *The Family in America, A Journal of Public Policy,* Fall 2009, at http://www.familyinamerica.org/pdf/FIA_fall09_CarlsonEssay.pdf.

151 Henry R. Van Til, *The Calvinistic Concept of Culture,* (Grand Rapids, Mich.: Baker Book House, 1972), p. 32.

152 William Meezan and Jonathan Rauch, "Gay Marriage, Same-sex Parenting, and America's Children," *The Future of Children* Vol. 15 No. 2 Marriage and Child Wellbeing (Autumn 2005), p. 102.

153 Preeti Dhillon, "A Survey of Cultural Values: Is a Universally Ethical Financial System Possible?" *Seven Pillars Institute Moral Cents* Vol. 2 Issue 2, Summer/Fall 2013, http://sevenpillarsinstitute.org/wp-content/uploads/2013/10/Survey-of-Values-Across-Cultures-EDITED.pdf (accessed February 17, 2016).

154 Political Advocacy Tracker, "Glenn Beck: 'Leave Your Church,'" *Christianity Today.com* March 12, 2010, at http://www.christianitytoday.com/ct/2010/marchweb-only/20-51.0.html.

155 Ibid.

156 Sojourners: Christians for Justice and Peace at http://www.google.com/search?sourceid=navclient&ie=UTF-8&rlz=1T4DKUS_enUS344&q=sojourners.

157 Sojourners' Mission at website: Sojourners: Faith, Politics, Culture, at http://www.sojo.net/index.cfm?action=about_us.mission.

158 D. James Kennedy, "The Bible and Economics," in *The Mortgaging of America,* (Coral Ridge Ministries Media, Inc., 2009), p. 15.

159 D. James Kennedy, "Does the Bible Teach Socialism?" in *The Mortgaging of America,* (Ft. Lauderdale, FL: Coral Ridge Ministries Media, Inc., 2009), p. 39.

160 Ibid., p. 42.

161 Robert Knight, *Radical Rulers: The White House Elites Who Are Pushing America Toward Socialism,* (Ft. Lauderdale, FL: Coral Ridge Ministries Media, Inc., 2010), p. 29.

162 Anthony B. Bradley, "The Marxist Roots of Black Liberation Theology," Acton Institute, April 2, 2008, at http://www.acton.org/commentary/443_marxist_roots_of_black_liberation_theology.php. Quoted in *Radical Rulers* by Robert Knight (Ft. Lauderdale, FL: Coral Ridge Ministries Media, Inc., 2010), p. 30.

163 Ibid.

164 Tommy Newberry, *The War on Success: How the Obama Agenda Is Shattering the American Dream,* (Washington, D.C.: Regnery Publishing, Inc., 2010), p. 116.

165 Ronald H. Nash, *Poverty and Wealth: Why Socialism Doesn't Work,* (Richardson, TX: Probe Books, 1986), p. 11.

166 Ibid.

167 Frederic Bastiat, *The Law,* translated by Dean Russell, (Irving-on-Hudson, NY: The Foundation for Economic Education, Inc., 1998), p. 31.

168 Karl Marx and Friedrich Engels, *Manifesto of the Communist Party,* (Google Books), pp. 43-44, at http://books.google.com/books?id=s2iEeCJAIusC&dq=Karl+Marx+destroy+the+family&printsec=frontcover&source=in&hl=en&ei=-6tWCS720N86UtgfK_4HdBg&sa=X&oi=book_result&ct=result&resnum=11&ved=0CCQQ6AEwCg#v=onepage&q=&f=false

169 Joel McDurmon, *God Versus Socialism: Slavery and Sacrifice in Modern Government,* (Powder Springs, Ga.: American Vision Press, 2009), p. 53.

170 David Horowitz, *Radical Son: A Generational Odyssey,* (New York: Touchstone, 1997), p. 415.

171 Stéphane Courtois, Nicolas Werth, Jean-Louis Panné, Andrzej Paczkowski, Karel Bartošek, Jean-Louis Margolin, *The Black Book of Communism: Crimes, Terror, Repression,* trans. Jonathan Murphy and Mark Kramer, (Cambridge, Mass: The President and Fellows of Harvard College, 1999), pp. 412-413, at http://www.amazon.com/Black-Book-Communism-Crimes Repression/dp/0674076087/ref=sr_1_1?ie=UTF

8&s=books&qid=1268755886&sr=1-1#reader_0674076087.

172 Richard Wurmbrand, "Haters of God," *The Voice of the Martyrs Magazine*, March 2010, p. 10, at www. persecution.com.

173 McDurmon, *God vs. Socialism,* p. 53.

174 Harry Farley, "Open Doors: Syria and Iraq are 'the tip of the iceberg' – there has never been a worse time to be a Christian," *ChristianityToday.com*, January 13, 2016, http://www.christiantoday.com/article/open.doors.syria.and.iraq.are.the.tip.of.the.iceberg.there.has.never.been.a.worse.time.to.be.a.christian/76374.htm?email=1 (accessed February 12, 2016).

175 Open Doors World Watch List 2016 North Korea Fact Sheet, https://www.opendoorsusa.org/christian-persecution/world-watch-list/north-korea/ (accessed February 11, 2016).

176 World Watch List 2010: *An In-depth Look at Persecution Around the World*, Open Doors USA, at http://members.opendoorsusa.org/site/PageServer?pagename=World_Watch_List_2010

177 Open Doors World Watch List 2016, https://*www.opendoorsusa.org/christian-persecution/world-watch-list/* (accessed February 11, 2016).

178 "World Report 2015: China," Human Rights Watch, https://www.hrw.org/world-report/2015/country-chapters/china-and-tibet (accessed February 17, 2016).

179 Courtois et al., *The Black Book of Communism,* p. 4.

180 Herbert F. Meyer, "Bruce Walker's *The Swastika Against the Cross,*" American Thinker, April 4, 2009, at http://www.americanthinker.com/2009/04/bruce_walkers_the_swastika_aga_1.html.

181 Os Guinness, *The Great Experiment, Faith and Freedom in America* (Colorado Springs: NavPress, 2001), 25-26, quoted in *Saving Freedom* by Jim DeMint, (Nashville, TN: B&H Publishing, 2009), p. 154.

182 Gary MacEoin, *Unlikely Allies: The Christian-Socialist Convergence*, (New York: Crossroad Publishing Co., 1990), p. xii.

183 Peter Foster, "Venezuela's 'socialist paradise' turns into a nightmare: medical shortages claim lives as oil price collapses," *The Telegraph*, February 3, 2015, http://www.telegraph.co.uk/news/worldnews/southamerica/venezuela/11385294/Venezuelas-socialist-paradise-turns-into-a-nightmare-medical-shortages-claim-lives-as-oil-price-collapses.html (accessed February 17, 2016).

184 "Hugo Chavez," *Encyclopedia Britannica*, www.britannica.com/biography/Hugo-Chavez (accessed February 15, 2016).

185 Foster, "Venezuela's 'socialist paradise.'"

186 "Hispanics of Venezuelan Origin in the United States, 2013," *Pew Research Center, Hispanic Trends,* September 10, 2015, http://www.pewhispanic.org/2015/09/15/hispanics-of-venezuelan-origin-in-the-united-states-2013/ph_2015-09-15_hispanic-origins-venezuela-01/ (accessed February 15, 2016).

187 Victor Andres, *Fleeing Castro: Operation Pedro Pan and the Cuban Children's Program*, (Gainesville, Fla.: University Press of Florida, 1998), p. xiii.

188 Ibid.

189 Monsignor Bryan O. Walsh, "The History of Operation Pedro Pan," Pedropan.org, March 1, 2001, at http://www.pedropan.org/history.html.

190 Robert F. Gorman, *Historical Dictionary of Refugee and Disaster Relief Organizations*, (Metuchen, N.J.: The Scarecrow Press, Inc., 1994), p. 143.

191 Ibid.

192 "Cuba" *Wikipedia*, https://en.wikipedia.org/wiki/Cuba (accessed 2/15/2016).

193 (UNHCR) United Nations High Commissioner of Refugees 2000, *The State of the World's Refugees*, (New York: Oxford University Press, 2000), p. 121.

194 Gorman, p. 154.

195 Ibid.

196 Ibid., p. 155.

197 UNHCR, United Nations, State of the Refugees, p. 15.

198 Ibid.

199 Walter Laqueur, *Generation Exodus: The Fate of Young Jewish Refugees from Nazi Germany*, (Hanover, N.H.: University Press of New England, 2001), p. 24.

200 Ibid., p. 27.

201 United States Holocaust Memorial Museum, at http://www.ushmm.org/wlc/article.php?ModuleId=10005139.

202 http://en.wikipedia.org/wiki/Uprising_of_1953_in_East_Germany.

203 Jennifer A. Yoder, *From East Germans to Germans? The New Postcommunist Elites*, (Durham, N.C.: Duke University Press, 1999), p. 47.

204 Ibid.

205 Mary Fulbrook, *A Concise History of Germany*, (New York, NY: Cambridge University Press, 1990), p. 234.

206 Yoder, *From East Germans*, p. 54.

207 Michelle E. Houle, *The Vietnamese*, (Farmington Hills., Mich.: Greenhaven Press, 2000), p. 28.

208 UNHCR, United Nations, State of the Refugees, p. 81.

209 Ibid.

210 Ibid., p. 82.

211 Gorman, p. 168.

212 UNHCR, United Nations, State of the Refugees, p. 90.

213 "Kim Il-sung," *Wikipedia*, https://en.wikipedia.org/wiki/Kim_Il-sung (accessed February 15, 2016).

214 "Mass-Starvations in North Korea," *NorthKoreaNow.org*, http://www.northkoreanow.org/the-crisis/mass-starvations-in-north-korea/ (accessed February 17, 2016).

215 "Report: N. Korea building fence to keep people in," The Associated Press, as reported in *The Houston Chronicle*, August 26, 2007, at http://www.chron.com/disp/story.mpl/front/5084232.html.

216 Ibid.

217 Steven Lear, "I'm Not Ready to Die . . . Yet," *Voice of the Martyrs*, March 2010.

218 Cheryl K. Chumley, "Kim Jong-un Calls for Execution of 33 Christians," *The Washington Times*, March 6, 2014, http://www.washingtontimes.com/news/2014/mar/6/kim-jong-un-calls-execution-33-christians/ (accessed February 15, 2016).

219 Janet Porter, "Austria in the '30s: Mirror to America," WorldNetDaily.com, September 22, 2009, at http://www.wnd.com/index.php?pageId=110602.

220 Alexander Solzhenitsyn, "A World Split Apart," Commencement Address at Harvard University, June 8, 1978, at: http://www.columbia.edu/cu/augustine/arch/solzhenitsyn/harvard1978.html.

221 Alexander Solzhenitsyn, quoted in Edward E. Ericson, Jr., "Solzhenitsyn: Voice from the Gulag," *Eternity*, October 1985, pp. 23–24.

222 Coral Ridge Ministries interview with Rep. Michele Bachmann on Feb. 5, 2010.

223 D. James Kennedy, "Amerika: Another Option," sermon preached March 18, 1987. (Fort Lauderdale, FL: Coral Ridge Ministries).

ABOUT THE AUTHORS

John Aman is a writer and communications consultant with more than two decades of experience serving some of the nation's leading Christian, conservative, and pro-life organizations. He is the author of dozens of articles and books on current issues including, *Ten Truths About Hate Crime Laws* and *The Obamacare Death Panel: The Powerful Unelected Board That Threatens Your Healthcare.*

Robert H. Knight is a Senior Fellow for the American Civil Rights Union and a *Washington Times* contributor. His books include *Radical Rulers: The Washington Elites Who Are Pushing America Toward Socialism, Fighting for America's Soul: How Sweeping Change Threatens Our Nation and What We Can Do.*

Andrew Scott is a writer and editor with writing and research experience is a wide range of areas including Christian ministry, education, radio communications, and the business sector.

Karen VanTil Gushta, Ph.D., has an earned doctorate in Philosophy of Education, and is a writer and editor at D. James Kennedy Ministries. She has written a number of books published by the ministry including, *The War on Children* and *Common Core: Better Education or Educational Child Abuse?*

▶ RESOURCES TO HELP YOU LEARN MORE!

The Problem of Socialism

Wherever socialism rules—freedom is the first casualty, crushed under the heavy hand of the state. Socialism's demagogues promise a utopian, atheistic heaven on earth, but only bring misery and suffering.

The DVD, *The Problem of Socialism*, shows the dangers of socialism at a time when it is on the march in America. Learn how the ideas of socialism's founders and followers violate God's Word and have brought slavery and death to tens and even hundreds of millions wherever they have been tried.

DVD (720178)

▶ RESOURCES TO HELP YOU LEARN MORE!

Social Justice: *How Good Intentions Undermine Justice and Gospel*

One of the foremost evangelical experts on economic and environmental issues today, Dr. E. Calvin Beisner, explains how well-meaning Christians are being duped by those promoting an unbiblical agenda to redistribute wealth under the name of "social justice."

Booklet (115859)

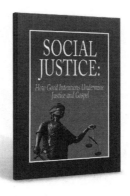

► RESOURCES TO HELP YOU LEARN MORE!

America at the Tipping Point

Is there hope for America? Are we letting the Christian heritage of our nation slip through our finders? Is it too late to reverse the course our nation is taking and return it to our true roots in the principles of biblical Christianity?

In this set of seven sermons, available on both CD and DVD, Dr. D. James Kennedy addresses these questions with inspiring messages such as the following:

- America: A Christian Nation
- America's Greatest Hero
- God and Country
- Spirit of Liberty
- America for God (which was a speech delivered at the Lincoln Memorial)
- America Adrift
- Returning to Our Roots

7-CD set (740226)
7-DVD set (720069)

For these and other resources available from
D. James Kennedy Ministries, visit

www.DJamesKennedy.org
or call **1-800-988-7884**